AMAZING AND EXTRAORDINARY FACTS

TITANIC

TITANIC

STUART ROBERTSON

RP
RYDON
PUBLISHING

CONTENTS

INTRODUCTION

'*Titanic*, name and thing, will stand as a monument and warning to human presumption.' – The Bishop of Winchester, preaching in Southampton, 1912

In a curtain call of history's great maritime disasters, *Titanic* dominates the stage. At first her name evokes images of towering bows, sweeping lines and imposing funnels, beautiful interiors and elegant passengers. But as the light fades and the temperature drops ominously, the ship's stately progress turns into a nightmarish montage of scenes of complacency, confusion, panic, and eventually the loss of more than 1,500 lives along with the pride of the White Star Line, supposedly unsinkable. The *Titanic* disaster is not the largest at sea in terms of lives lost or tonnage of vessel sunk. But it is undoubtedly the most stirring and well-known. Why?

Because the story has all the elements of high drama, tragedy, heroism, hubris, humanity and, at times, grim comedy, guaranteed to connect with anyone who chooses to engage with the events of 14–15 April 1912. *Titanic*'s sheer size and state-of-the-art engineering, reputation for unsinkability, her owners' pride and the desire of the rich and famous to take passage on her maiden voyage created the circumstances for one of the world's great ironic mishaps. Furthermore, at every stage the *Titanic*'s story is a highly sensory tale – from the industrious clanging of the ironworkers in the shipyard of her birth, the feel of the plush carpeting and panelling of the smoking rooms and libraries, the steady thrum and throb of the engines, the clinking glassware and chattering of the passengers sitting down to a sumptuous dinner, to the terrifying sight of the looming wall of ice and the adrenaline-filled surge of the panicked crowds as the stern rises before the final plunge, while the ship's musicians play on – many of the key elements of the ship's life and death lend themselves to vivid reconstruction in our fascinated imaginations. It is also a disaster which in recent years has hovered just out of reach of modern memory, endowing it with a heightened air of symbolism and romanticism buoyed by the work of cinematographers and fiction writers. If a disaster can be said to have 'popular appeal', then *Titanic* steals the show.

2012 was the centenary of the *Titanic*'s sinking. From today's vantage point we are encouraged to believe that we know better than to let a ship steam at speed into an ice field at night. With the cushion of a century it is perhaps natural to think we know all the answers to the questions churned up by the loss of the *Titanic* – that the lessons learned were tragically obvious in hindsight. We might feel justified in thinking less of those who weren't able to see trouble coming out of the gloom on that still, moonless night. And certainly the events of the night throw up examples of the best and worst of human behaviour under stress. But that is to judge history's people and processes by different standards. It is easy to be wise after the event.

Nevertheless, *Titanic*'s loss changed the rules for passenger ships of all sizes; never again would the world's leading shipping lines belonging to the wealthiest nations on earth take such risks with the safety of sea-going passengers during peacetime. Her loss also seemed in hindsight to herald a new era of turmoil, as American survivor Jack B Thayer remembered: 'There was peace and the world had an even tenor to its way... It seems to me that the disaster about to occur was the event that not only made the world rub its eyes and awake but woke it with a start keeping it moving at a rapidly accelerating pace ever since with less and less peace, satisfaction and happiness. To my mind the world of today awoke April 15th, 1912.'

A mere five days before, on the afternoon of 10 April 1912, as the *Titanic* slowly bore away with the assistance of tugs from the quayside at Southampton, it is tempting to think that two thousand souls each spent a few moments contemplating what the coming days aboard the world's biggest and most luxurious new liner would bring. For some the journey was simply a necessity of business; for others, part of the intercontinental social whirl; for many it was another day at work in the machinery spaces or in the corridors, lounges and restaurants of the opulently appointed liner; for others it was to be the start of a whole new life in the New World. Among the bright lights and the comfortable surrounds, the hustle and bustle of embarkation and the petty dramas and excitements of exploring a new ship, how many could have foreseen that in a little over one hundred hours' time three quarters of their number would be dead and adrift on the freezing Atlantic, and the world's largest moving object – the apotheosis of human engineering achievement, wrought in iron and crewed by master mariners – would lie broken up in stone cold pitch darkness 12,000 feet down on the sea bed, never to reach her destination a thousand miles away?

Harland and Wolff:
Belfast's steely identity
The birthplace of Titanic

Situated at the head of Belfast Lough, about 11 miles from the open sea, Ulster's first city has been building ships on a commercial basis for over three centuries. No other city in the British Isles has been so dominated by a single industry. It's in the blood, and in its heyday one particular shipbuilder came to symbolise the whole city of Belfast. During the Victorian period the growth of Belfast's key industry was influenced by Liverpool's rise as a maritime hub for imperial exports and imports. In 1853 Robert Hickson decided to locate his iron shipbuilding business on Queen's Island, one of three artificial islands newly created in the recently dredged River Lagan, which leads into the centre of Belfast. For five years he concentrated on building ships for Liverpool and Ulster merchants but the business was not a success. In what would today amount to a management buyout, Yorkshireman Edward Harland – a manager at the yard – and his marine draughtsman assistant Gustav Wolff, a German Jew from Hamburg, joined forces and took control of the business under the patronage of Wolff's uncle G C Schwabe, a prominent Liverpool-based merchant of great wealth and connections. As Liverpool expanded and prospered as Britain's principal west-coast trading centre, the new Harland and Wolff yard looked to supply the demand emanating from across the St George's Channel. Schwabe's influence was crucial. Connected to a number of key business figures and shipping lines he was able to generate orders for the ground-breaking yard; it is reputed that during a game of billiards

*Gustav Wolff and
Edward Harland*

at his home, Schwabe persuaded the owner of the newly reformed Liverpool-based White Star Line – one Thomas Henry Ismay, father of the man who would order the *Titanic* – to place his orders for ships with the cutting-edge Harland and Wolff outfit, in return for assistance with financing the reborn line.

From Liverpool to Southampton via bankruptcy
The White Star Line's chequered history

The original White Star Line was founded in Liverpool and concentrated on routes between the UK and Australia. The company bought its first steamship in 1863, but went bust four years later, owing £527,200 (approximately £35 million today). Thomas Ismay

– a director of a rival shipping line – bought the trading rights and house flag in 1868. His immediate priority was to form a strong business relationship with Harland and Wolff and its sponsor Schwabe. In doing so, in 1869 Ismay and Harland and Wolff agreed to go ahead on a new fleet of *Oceanic* class ships to service the North Atlantic trade between New York and Liverpool. To operate this new fleet Ismay established the Oceanic Steam Navigation Company Ltd, while retaining the White Star Line name and flag for practical purposes.

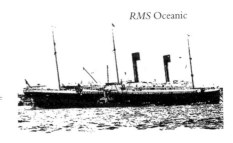
RMS Oceanic

THE *OCEANIC* EXPERIMENT
*Harland and Wolff's first ship for the White Star Line was the 3,800-ton ship **Oceanic**, launched in*

1871. She represented a significant evolution of the vessels already plying the burgeoning transatlantic routes. Designed from the outset as a passenger-only liner, she incorporated a number of innovations in speed, accommodation, layout and passenger comfort, setting aside no space for commercial freight. Her designers took the step of having the usual separate wooden deckhouses combined into a single structure extending along most of the ship's length. Old-fashioned sailing-ship solid bulwarks were replaced with an open metal deck railing and a neat row of stanchions supporting an accommodation deck above. This arrangement represented probably the most visibly obvious change in ship design since paddle wheels had disappeared in favour of the screw propeller – for the first time the basis of the modern liner's configuration had been made manifest.
Below decks the vessel's machinery grew more complex in order to cater for additional services. Evaporators and distillation plants were added to provide desalinated water for boiler and domestic supplies.

Able to make a crossing to the US at an average speed of 14 knots, she was a triumph for shipbuilder and operator and set the bar high for competitors.

The relationship between White Star and Harland and Wolff quickly became very close. Each enterprise held shares in the other. In 1873 the company suffered a major disaster when the SS *Atlantic* sank near Halifax, Nova Scotia, with the loss of over 500 lives. In 1891 Thomas Ismay made his son Joseph Bruce Ismay a partner in the firm, and a year later, with his health failing, Thomas resigned. J Bruce Ismay took over White Star.

Between 1870 and the outbreak of the First World War in 1914 the Belfast yard – occupying a sophisticated, integrated ship construction site of 95 acres and employing over 10,000 skilled tradesmen – was able to deliver to the White Star line over sixty ships totalling three quarters of a million tons. White Star quickly adopted as tradition ship names ending in '-ic'. (Similarly, rival Cunard went for '-ia'.)

These, along with its house flag, the red burgee, made the line's vessels easily recognisable to the travelling public. In the last two decades of the nineteenth century, the White Star Line operated many famous ships, such as *Britannic, Germanic, Teutonic* and *Majestic*. Several of these ships became successful record-breakers, some taking the Blue Riband for the line.

In 1899 Ismay commissioned the second *Oceanic*, lauded as one of the most beautiful steam ships built during the nineteenth century. She was the first ship to exceed Brunel's *Great Eastern* in length. The building of *Oceanic* marked a departure in policy for White Star: speed was out – comfort, size and economy of operation were in.

Bruce
Ismay

Building for comfort not speed
Blue Riband takes a back seat

Since its beginnings in the 1830s, there have been 35 transatlantic liner holders of what eventually became known as the Blue Riband, each notching up a few extra knots or shaving off a few hours at sea to enter the transatlantic record books. Twenty-five holders were British, with five German, three American, one French and one Italian. Britain's Cunard liners took the most honours – thirteen – against five holders owned by White Star and four by German line Norddeutscher Lloyd. For a period in the later years of the nineteenth and early twentieth centuries, the desire for speed became an obsession. Norddeutscher even returned one of its new liners, the *Kaiser Friedrich*, to her builders when it was discovered that the ship would not make her contract speed. But in the race to commission ever-quicker passenger ships, some lines found that passengers cared less about getting to New York or Boston a day earlier if that meant sacrificing comfort and smooth sailing. In the days before stabilizers and bilge keels, ships built for speeds of more than 20 knots could suffer from unwelcome vibration and instability in heavy seas, and devoted less space to lucrative passenger amenities.

White Star dropped out of the running and instead decided to concentrate on bigger, more luxurious vessels which did not push at the boundaries of speed but instead made more room for the big spenders and the mass emigration trade. Meanwhile, in 1909 Cunard's *Mauretania* smashed the record by gunning across the Atlantic at an average speed of 26.06 knots – not far short of the quickest naval warships of the day – and established a record which stood for the next two decades. Even so, for its next superliner – the *Aquitania*, launched in 1914 – Cunard opted for size and luxury over outright speed. Many of the big transatlantic liners were requisitioned by national governments for use as troop-carriers and armed merchantmen during the First World War, and several were lost, including the *Lusitania* which in May 1915 was

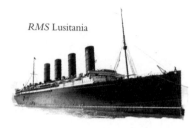

RMS Lusitania

torpedoed by the German submarine *U-20* off Old Head of Kinsale in southern Ireland, sinking with the loss of 1,198 lives.

The *Titanic* and her sister ships *Olympic* and *Britannic* were never designed to compete for the Blue Riband. Instead their designers and builders put size, technology and luxury ahead of speed. But even so *Titanic* was no slouch. Capable of a top speed of 22 knots (1 knot = 1 nautical mile an hour = 1.1 land miles an hour = 0.51 metres per second) she was half as big again as the *Lusitania* yet comparable in speed to the record breakers of the nineteenth century (and a bit faster than the flat-out speed of today's top 200m sprinters), driven forward by two sets of four cylinder triple-expansion reciprocating steam engines turning the port and starboard propeller shafts at 15,000 indicated horse power (IHP) each. *Titanic* featured a third propeller shaft located at the aft end of her keel centreline, and this was driven by a low-pressure Parsons steam turbine feeding off the steam created by the other two engines, thereby generating 16,000 horsepower. To feed her powerplants, *Titanic* consumed 825 tons of coal a day, relatively economic compared to consumption required by the swifter Cunard boats.

The last holder of the Blue Riband before the jet age stole the transatlantic passenger market – the American liner *United States* – was able to cross the Atlantic at a comfortable 31 knots on 158,000 horsepower in the 1950s. On her maiden voyage in 1952 she crossed westbound in an incredible three days, 12 hours and 12 minutes at an average speed of 34.51 knots, thereby smashing the record of 30.99 knots and three days, 21 hours and 48 minutes previously set by Britain's Cunarder *Queen Mary* in 1938. Built to US Navy specifications as a dual-use liner able to transport 14,000 troops in time of war, the *United States* was rumoured to be capable of a maximum speed of 40 knots while generating 240,000 shaft horsepower through four compound triple-expansion turbine sets, with double-reduction gearing to the propeller shafts. That's nearly 70 feet per second!

American-financed, American-owned...
How British was Titanic?

The old guard of the late nineteenth century liner industry in Britain changed upon the death in 1895 of Sir Edward Harland the Belfast shipbuilding tycoon, followed in 1899 by the passing of Thomas Henry Ismay of the White Star Line. At the same time, the enormous cost of constructing and maintaining expanding fleets of ever-bigger ocean liners began to press upon the industry. Smaller lines were bought out and the larger companies sought amalgamation to remain competitive. In tandem with this consolidation came the need to seek financial input from new sources. Principal among these was American finance.

In 1902 the International

Mercantile Marine Company was founded by American shipping magnates, absorbing a number of smaller British and American concerns and backed by the monetary muscle of JP Morgan. To the surprise and consternation of the shipping industry and the British government, the White Star Line's new chairman and managing director – Joseph Bruce Ismay, son of Thomas Henry – was revealed as a significant player on the IMMC's board, although he had been against the move originally. In 1904 Ismay was persuaded by White Star shareholders to take the IMMC presidency. By 1902 only the British company Cunard and the French line Compagnie Générale Transatlantique were independent of the IMMC.

Cunard's fears about the dominance of the new giant US-owned shipping conglomerate were never fully realised – only White Star, with its fleet of large ships and its prestige, consistently turned a profit for the combine – but were echoed in British political circles and encouraged a British government subsidy to Cunard to build ships to rival White Star's 'Big Four' (*Celtic,*

Cedric, Baltic, Adriatic) of the early twentieth century. Once approved, Cunard received an annual subsidy of £150,000 and a low interest loan of £2.5 million to build what would become the *Lusitania* and *Mauretania.* British maritime prestige – not to mention auxiliary armed merchantmen and fast troop-carrying capacity if war should come – was considered to be at stake.

IT'S NOT FAIR PLAY

As worried British commentators observed, the fact that White Star liners flew British flags did little to conceal the truth that to all intents and purposes they were American owned and American operated ships dominating the transatlantic routes, as this letter to **Fairplay** *magazine in 1905 spelt out: 'What most people do feel is the keenest regret that such a magnificent line as the White Star… aggregating nearly one million tons of our best shipping, should have passed from British to American control. The Combine fleets are American to the backbone; Americans found the capital, and it is Americans who appoint and pay the managers* *on this side. It is nothing but a mere pretence to say that through the technical wording of the Company's Act they are in any sense British, though through this technicality they are allowed to fly the British flag, a fact which most people regard as nothing less than a public scandal.'*

Effectively then, by the time *Titanic* emerged she was an American vessel. However, Morgan kept the ships run by the IMMC under British registry with British crews. He did this in order to avoid breaking the terms of the American Sherman Anti-Trust Act of 1890, a piece of legislation which had spectacularly affected John D Rockefeller's dominant Standard Oil Company which was broken up by the Supreme Court in 1911. Most of White Star's ships flew both American and British flags along with the White Star Line corporate flag.

Harland and Wolff's new boss, Lord Pirrie, was also concerned that his main customer was now controlled largely by American interests. Ismay sought to reassure Pirrie that the Belfast shipyard was still first port of call for White Star – and with the

line's ambitious plans to dominate the North Atlantic passenger routes would come the need to conceive and build a truly world-beating series of giant ships. The launch in September 1907 of Cunard's subsidised super-ships *Lusitania* and *Mauretania* upped the pressure. In the board room of the rival White Star line and the drawing rooms of Pirrie's yard, plans were drawn to stake a renewed claim for glory. In July 1908 a contract was signed for three giant new liners. But sheer size and opulence and not speed would be the yardsticks by which the White Star Line would measure its future.

Heavy metal
The Olympic *class on the stocks*

With £3 million secured for the building of two new liners, on 16 December 1908 the keel for Ship No. 400 – later to become the *Olympic* – was laid down on a specially constructed slipway in Harland and Wolff's yard, followed by Ship No. 401, the *Titanic*, on 31 March 1909. The Belfast yard underwent huge modification

Titanic *and* Olympic

piers in New York had to be extended by over 100 feet to accommodate their unprecedented length.

The *Olympic* was started first and she came out of the blocks on 20 October 1910 to much fanfare. As the lead ship of a planned trio her launch and fitting-out marked the start of a huge publicity campaign to attract the public. Interviews were given to the press, and trade journals took a huge interest in the ground-breaking specifications. The day that *Olympic* left Belfast as a complete ship – 31 May 1911 – was, by happy coincidence for White Star, the same day that *Titanic* would be launched. It was also the joint birthday of Lord and Lady Pirrie of Harland and Wolff.

in order to accommodate the simultaneous construction of the two new giants, including the construction of a new graving dock, the Thompson dock. A brand new gantry, the Arrol – the biggest in the world at 6,000 tons – was specially built over the new slipways to act as a massive scaffolding platform. The yard workforce expanded by 100 per cent to over 11,000 men, paid on average £2 for a hard 49-hour week. Over 24,000 tons of steel would be used to build the hull and the superstructure of each ship. A 200-ton floating crane was procured from Germany to lift heavy objects like engines and boilers into the hull. Southampton harbour was dredged in anticipation of the size of these new ships, and the White Star

RMS Olympic

Slip sliding away
Launch day

The Harland and Wolff slipway from which the *Titanic* was launched into Belfast Lough at 12:13 on 31 May 1911 still exists. From the moment the wooden triggers holding her in place were released, it took 62 seconds for the immense hull to slide backwards the full length of the slip and to come to rest in the roiling, chilly water, watched by 100,000 people. Observers calculated she had picked up a fair bit of speed, possibly as much as 12 knots, on the way to taking her first dip in the sea. But thanks to the heavy dragging chains attached to her she safely came to rest within about her own length.

Dock workers had spent days before the launch greasing the slipway. Over twenty tons of tallow (animal fat), train oil and soap were spread an inch thick all along the slipway down which the *Titanic* slid that day. To our eyes, accustomed to thinking of the ship in all her glory, the freshly-launched hull would have looked remarkably bare. There were no funnels visible, no paint scheme, no blazing lights, and no interior fittings, just the enormous riveted steel hulk settling in the sea.

RIVETING STUFF
Three million rivets – made from 1500 tons of metal – were used in the construction of **Titanic**. *Made of steel and wrought iron, they were used to attach steel plates either to each other or to a steel frame (which was itself held together by other rivets). The concept is simple and rather like Meccano with added heat: make holes in the steel plates and correspondingly in the frame. Heat up the rivet until its chemical composition changes from ferrite to austenite (you'll need about 1,100 degrees Celsius for that) and it becomes soft and malleable, and then insert it into the relevant paired holes. Squeeze it until it fills the hole and a head is formed on both sides. Only another 2,999,999 to go! In addition to riveting, the shipbuilders also took advantage of the technique of welding when they fitted the two expansion joints whose job it was to manage the stress on the hull caused by longitudinal flexing.*

However, neither riveted or welded joints could have withstood the stresses the hull would eventually be subjected to.

Men whose livelihood depends on the sea are a superstitious breed. There was no christening ceremony for *Titanic* in Belfast. As one of the yard workers was reputedly heard to say at the launch of *Britannic*, 'They just builds her and shoves her in!'

MRS ISMAY'S PERSONAL NAMING CEREMONY

In spite of there being no official christening for Yard Number 401, Mrs Florence Ismay, wife of White Star chairman J Bruce Ismay, was reported to have said quietly, 'I name this ship the **Titanic**, *and may God bless her and all who sail in her', as she watched the vessel slide down the slip. Somewhere else in the crowd, a White Star employee was overheard to say, 'Not even God himself could sink this ship'. For the superstitious out there, could this have been the source of* **Titanic** *'s bad luck?*

When the *Titanic* was launched a workman was seriously injured by a support he was cutting away, and later died of his injuries in hospital. According to one *Titanic* expert, any shipbuilding yard could expect to lose one man killed for every 10,000 tons of shipping built and launched. Upon launch, the brand-new vessel was towed to another part of the dockyard, where the ten-month construction of her luxurious interior could begin in earnest.

It's big
Largest moving man-made object on Earth

In stark terms, *Titanic's* vitals were: length – 882.75 feet; beam (width) – 92.5 feet; draft (depth below the waterline) – 34.5 feet; height from keel to top of the exhaust stacks – 175 feet; height from waterline to the boat deck – 60 feet. She weighed 46,328 gross tons. So how does this compare with other ships of similar purpose or period?

Compared in general to the famous Cunard paddle steamer *Britannia* – a pioneer of the transatlantic route of the 1840s – *Titanic* was ten times heavier, four times as long, twice as deep below the waterline, three times as broad, carried twenty times the number of passengers and ten times the crew. *Titanic* steamed comfortably at two and a half times the speed of *Britannia* thanks to engines which generated over sixty times the amount of horsepower available to the Cunarder's paddles. *Britannia* would look like a steam yacht by comparison if she had ever run alongside the Belfast brute (she was sunk as a target ship in 1880).

Titanic was half as heavy again as the Clydebank-built *Lusitania* launched five years earlier, showing a hundred feet more length, five feet more beam and a little less draft. Her extra size meant she was able to provide superior accommodation for everyone she carried, not least the extra 350 lucrative First- and Second-class passengers she had room for – and this was where the real money was to be made for any serious shipping line wishing to make profits.

Titanic was the largest moving object on Earth at the time, bigger even than many static land-built constructions. She was four fifths the height of The Shard, the tallest building in London. In its day, by comparison, the world's tallest skyscraper (completed in 1913) was Cass Gilbert's Woolworth Building in New York, standing in at only 793 feet (242 metres)! The tallest building in the British empire at the time was the Sun Tower in Vancouver, Canada, at a mere 269 feet (82 metres). Today's RMS *Queen Mary 2,* the world's biggest-ever passenger ocean liner and Cunard's modern flagship, is 345 metres in length and weighs 151,400 gross tonnes. She is capable

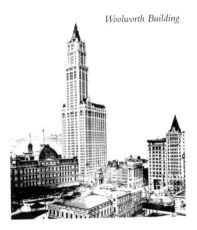

Woolworth Building

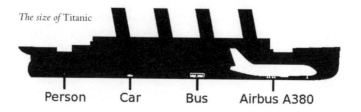

The size of Titanic

Person   Car   Bus   Airbus A380

of 30 knots though her normal service speed is 26 knots – still a good few knots faster than the bulkier cruise ships. The biggest cruise ship to date is the enormous *Symphony of the Seas* (RCI), constructed in 2018 and is 362.1m, 228,081 tonnes, holds 6680 passengers and travels at 22 knots.

The *Titanic* was nearly as long as four huge Airbus A380 airliners laid end to end, which are a mere 238 feet in length each. By the standards of today, let alone those of a century ago, the *Titanic* was extremely aptly named.

WHAT'S IN A NAME?

Titanic: *Of or relating to the Titans. a. Having great stature or enormous strength; huge or colossal. b. Of enormous scope, power, or influence.*

In Greek mythology, the Titans were a race of powerful deities, descendants of Gaia and Uranus, who ruled during the legendary Golden Age. There has not been a rush to give many other ships the name **Titanic**, *for obvious reasons. As far as we know, one* **Titanic**, *a freighter, preceded the White Star Line's leviathan by 23 years. She was also Belfast-built but a tiddler in comparison at 1,608 gross tons. She was sold by her owners to a Chilean company in 1903, whereupon her name was changed. According to reports, there was probably a Latvian tanker of 22,000 tons* *launched in the mid-1960s which was renamed* Titanic *some time before her breaking up in the 1990s.*

Ill-starred sister?
The Olympic *and the origins of the 'unsinkable' description*

Although nothing tops the era-defining tragedy of the *Titanic*, her sister ship and precursor the *Olympic* suffered more than her fair share of very public mishaps. On 21 June 1911, as she was nursed by twelve tugboats into her berth in New York harbour at the end of her maiden transatlantic voyage, the force of *Olympic's* huge propellers dragged one of the tugs, the *O. L. Halenbeck*, hard underneath her stern, causing over $10,000-worth of damage to the tug. *Olympic* shrugged the incident off with barely more than a few scratch marks in her paint. Three months later she would get away much less lightly. Under the command of Captain Edward J Smith – though being directed by a local harbour pilot – the *Olympic* was exiting the Solent on 20 September on her way to her fifth Atlantic crossing when she was

accidentally rammed and seriously damaged by the British armoured cruiser HMS *Hawke* of nearly 8,000 tons, under the command of the aptly named Commander Blunt. The crash resulted in the flooding of two of *Olympic's* compartments and a twisted propeller shaft, but she was able to return to Southampton under her own power. Some commentators thought the Royal Navy commander was show-boating and got it wrong. Questioned on the matter some months later, Captain Edward Smith would not be drawn as to his opinion on the probable negligence of the Navy but offered the following assessment of the 'survivability' of the White Star's big liners:

'... the *Olympic* is unsinkable, and *Titanic* will be the same when she is put in commission... either of these vessels could be cut in halves and each half would remain afloat indefinitely. The non-sinkable vessel has been reached in these two wonderful craft.'

The night before he returned from New York to take command of the *Titanic* Smith told his dinner companions the same thing. The White Star veteran apparently said that he shared with the ship's designers the utmost confidence in her qualities, and declared that it was not possible for her to sink. He would be proved badly wrong very soon.

Olympic–Hawke *collision*

The epitome of safety at sea
Titanic*'s state of the art design philosophy*

Titanic was designed to carry the latest equipment to ensure her safe and efficient navigation on the high seas. In the event of calamity, she was designed to stay afloat indefinitely, more than long enough that help could arrive if it were needed – in effect, the public was encouraged to think of the vessel as one big lifeboat itself. The measures

that were designed to guarantee this included: fifteen watertight bulkheads, each closed either manually or by electrically powered doors controlled from the bridge and fitted with special water sensors; a double-bottom for extra protection and two bilge keels nearly 300 feet long which stuck out from the sides of the hull to encourage stability; a 5-kilowatt Marconi wireless set with a transmitting range of 500 miles; four 400-watt generators with extra back-ups; electric lights in every cabin and room; and a 50-telephone switchboard divided into two networks to enable swift and clear communication around the ship, both for crew and paying passengers.

The public marvelled at the press's reports of these new safety features, designed to allow the ship to remain afloat with two of her watertight compartments flooded. Since no-one could imagine anything more serious than a breach of that magnitude – like the *Olympic-Hawke* collision, rather than the unusually extended glancing blow sustained by the *Titanic*, opening up the first six compartments – the ship was deemed unsinkable.

To the public conditioned to believe in man's technological prowess, that bigger was better, the *Olympic* class's sheer size – even on paper – made them look invulnerable. As time wore on and publicity surrounding the marvels exceeded the expectations of even White Star's PR machine, the word 'practically' was more and more often omitted. Ismay preferred the slogan 'The largest and finest steamers in the world'.

Shipbuilders and shipowners are not usually in the business of creating hostages to fortune. Or are they? One female passenger booking a ticket for the maiden voyage enquired about insurance for her luggage, but was allegedly told by a White Star official that there was no need – why, the ship was unsinkable.

Both chief designer Thomas Andrews and Captain Smith were separately reported to have been overheard on the maiden voyage explaining that the ship could be 'cut crosswise into three pieces and each piece would float'. Even on the morning of 15 April, Philip Franklin, vice president of the White Star Line, stated to the throng assembled outside his New York office, 'We place absolute confidence in the *Titanic*. We believe that the boat is unsinkable.' It seems White Star really did believe their own hype.

The eerie foresight of Robertson and Stead
Predictions of the disaster?

There are several accounts of precognition and premonition associated with the *Titanic*. One psychiatrist working in the paranormal field in the 1960s recorded 19 incidents of premonitions experienced by would-be passengers within the fortnight before the ship departed Southampton. These included cancelled bookings after dreams about the disaster, or accounts by those who said it was bad luck to travel on a ship's maiden voyage.

But perhaps the most intriguing and substantial 'warning' of impending doom was issued a whole 14 years before the *Titanic*'s maiden voyage. In 1898 American author Morgan Robertson published a novel called *Futility, or The Wreck of the Titan*.

Robertson had spent time working at sea and wrote a number of fictional pieces based on his experiences. In addition he claimed to be a psychic. His story mirrors the true events of the *Titanic* tragedy closely, uncannily so. The *Titan* is a British-registered ship on a voyage across the Atlantic, scheduled for April. The *Titan* is so-called because it represents the last word in maritime size, power and technology: 'the largest craft afloat and the greatest of the works of men', no less. She displaces 70,000 tons; is 800 feet long; is triple-screwed; has a capacity of 3,000 people but is carrying 2,000; can make 24 knots; is equipped with 19 watertight bulkheads – and therefore deemed unsinkable – and carries 24 lifeboats, far too few for her capacity; and she is fatally damaged in a collision with an iceberg 400 miles from land!

Robertson's plot does not mirror the ship or the events completely, of course. The *Titan* has already crossed the ocean a few times before disaster strikes; she capsizes, rather than nosedives; her passage is augmented by sails, of which the *Titanic* had none. But oddly, elements of the story also presage real events which happened to the *Olympic*, in particular her collision with a fog-bound lightship in 1934.

In 1886, pioneering British social reformer, journalist, and part-time paranormalist William T Stead wrote an article which he published in the March edition of his magazine

Morgan Robertson

the *Pall Mall Gazette*. Titled 'How the Mail Steamer Went Down in the Mid-Atlantic, by a Survivor', it told of a large ship that sinks after a collision leading to large loss of life exacerbated by a lack of lifeboats. Stead emphasised that, 'This is exactly what might take place and what will take place if the liners are sent to sea short of boats.' Stead, a convinced spiritualist, also penned the 1892 story *From the Old World to the New*. In it he describes the sinking of a ship in the North Atlantic after collision with an iceberg. Eerily, in Stead's story, the captain of the ship *Majestic* which picks up the survivors is Edward Smith. Stead would die on the *Titanic*.

That is not all. In the *New York Times* of Tuesday 23 April 1912, an account of a memorial gathering to honour Stead contained an unsettling revelation by a Reverend Doctor Newell Dwight Hillis of Brooklyn. Friend and admirer of Stead's social activism, Hillis claimed that Stead had only recently predicted that his own death would not be peaceful. The article was subtitled 'Once Said He Would Never Die in His Bed, but in a Crowd, Struggling'.

A doomed ship?
Nonsense or truth?

Lots of odd stories have blossomed into life to help explain how – or why – the *Titanic* went down. It is easy to see how surviving passengers and the public might retrospectively ascribe reasons to account for the loss. After the event, many survivors reported weird feelings as they boarded the ship or left port, and so on. One female passenger was so convinced of the ship's jinx that she refused to sleep at night during the voyage. She was vindicated when she got away in a lifeboat. Even members of the crew afterwards claimed they had felt *Titanic* was not a 'happy ship'.

Disbelief at the tragedy readily combined with speculation and rumour to produce tales of bad luck and a 'doomed ship'. Sometimes these stories had started life much earlier but had been given new twists by the sinking. Perhaps the most famous example is the story of the mummy's curse.

The story goes that an Egyptian mummy – complete with obligatory late-19th century curse – had been sold by the British Museum to a sceptical American who arranged for it to be brought to the USA on the *Titanic*. Naturally, the curse struck the ship which duly sank. But the story's origins lie with one of the *Titanic*'s passengers who perished, William Stead (for it is he, again). A few years before, Stead had made up a story about an excavated mummy which had been bought by a friend. The mummy had been sold to a group of Englishmen, each of whom had gone on to suffer terrible bad luck, in some cases fatal. Having fed his invented story to the press before he left, Stead also recounted the fictional events to his dining companions aboard the *Titanic* on the night of the 13th. Stead's death on the *Titanic* – and the recollections of the only surviving dining companion – meant that the story became associated with the ship thereafter, even growing to encompass the incredible assertion that the mummy had been smuggled off the ship and onto the *Carpathia*! In truth, there was no mummy aboard ship.

Other stories have clung on over time. Some claimed that the ship was jinxed by the death of a trapped

docker. This story has probably been confused with those concocted to explain the problems which beset many other ships, notably Brunel's *Great Eastern*, launched in 1858. This pioneering liner was of hugely advanced design for its day, featuring an enormous double hull which would not be surpassed in length for another 40 years. Stories emerged of boy dockworkers becoming trapped in tight spaces while working down in the bowels of the ship. Older men reported hearing hammering noises long after workers had ceased toiling. A skeleton was rumoured to have been discovered when the ship was sent for scrap. Fortunately there is no official record of this, and certainly none with regard to *Titanic*.

A quick jaunt down the lough
Titanic*'s trials – and a baptism of fire?*

At dawn on Tuesday 2 April 1912 *Titanic* steamed out into Belfast Lough for her acceptance trials. These were a standard set of procedures designed to test the ship's

Titanic *trials*

play saw the ship describe a circle of 3,850 yards – nearly 2.2 miles!

Emergency stop drills were conducted, the ship coming to a halt after 850 yards. By 7 p.m. on 2 April the ship was back in Belfast, both anchors were dropped, and the Board of Trade's surveyor signed a certificate to say the ship was seaworthy and serviceable. Within the hour *Titanic* was off again, under the command of Captain Bartlett, in a hurry and heading for Southampton's midnight tide next day, carrying her first fare-paying customer, a Mr Van der Hoef who reportedly booked a First class ticket from Belfast to New York. Theoretically the carriage of this passenger would make Belfast the port from which *Titanic* departed on her maiden voyage. In any case, she would never see her birthplace again.

seaworthiness, responsiveness, speed, motion through the water, ability to stop, and general fitness for purpose. Aboard ship to observe, for the yard, were Edward Wilding and Thomas Andrews, chief designer, managing director and nephew of Lord Pirrie; representing the customer, White Star Line, was Harold. A. Sanderson; and in command was Captain Edward John Smith. A 'black gang' of 78 firemen, stokers and greasers and 41 crew members operated the ship.

The trials seem to have been conducted in a rather nonchalant way; they were done and dusted in a day. The new ship was worked up to 20 knots, cautiously at first, then her crew conducted steering tests using just her rudder and then her propellers. A full turn with both in

STOPPING AND STARTING

Titanic's *powerplants were simply awe-inspiring. She carried 29 coal stoked boilers, each of which was three storeys high and tended by firemen, stokers and engineers. Her four distinctive, enormous funnels were 62*

feet high and 22 feet wide. Three of them functioned as exhaust stacks for the boilers; the fourth, at the back, acted as a vent for the ship's many cooking areas. It also deliberately heightened the impressiveness of the ship's appearance. **Titanic***'s propulsion systems drove three enormous brass propellers. Two sat outside of the centreline, with one situated aft of the keel. The outside propellers weighed 38 tons and carried three ten-foot blades each, making a turning diameter of 23 feet; the centre propeller weighed 16 tons and had four six-foot blades with a diameter of 16 feet. At the other end of the ship – over 800 feet away – sat the* **Titanic***'s two anchors, each over 15 tons in weight. Each link in the anchor chains weighed 175 pounds! The rudder was a giant too, weighing in at over 100 tons.*

Inspecting a propeller

Intriguingly, the day before the trials took place a fire had broken out in the bunker between Nos 5 and 6 boiler rooms. Fires in coal bunkers were rare but not unheard of. This one is alleged to have buckled some of the plating which made up No. 5 watertight bulkhead. The fire burned for the first three days of the voyage, unbeknownst to the passengers and most of the crew. A fireman testified at the post-sinking British inquiry that he had helped put it out. He was asked what remedial work had then been done to the 'warped' metal. He replied, 'I just brushed it off and got some black oil and rubbed over it.' Despite Thomas Andrews's opinion at the inquiry that the fire was not big enough to seriously affect the watertight properties of the bulkhead, experts continue to believe it could have affected the integrity of the ship.

In fact, the ship was inspected by a representative of the Board of Trade's emigration department before she left port on the 10th. The fire was not reported. Some have argued that this was the last, missed, opportunity to stop an unready vessel from putting to sea. Questioned at the inquiry, the inspector admitted that his inspection routine was unsatisfactory. His excuse? 'Because it is the custom.' Asked if he followed custom even if it was bad, he replied, 'Well, you will remember I am a civil servant. Custom guides us a good bit.' Was this an indication of a culture of complacency surrounding the maiden voyage?

'Not very good material for a story'
The confident Captain Smith

Edward J. Smith

Edward J Smith was as close to a celebrity in his own lifetime as a ship's captain will ever come. Vastly experienced, sociable, erudite, reliable – a veritable firm hand on the tiller – the 'Millionaire's Captain' postponed his retirement to be able to take *Titanic* out on her maiden voyage. For the directors of the White Star Line, this was an eminently suitable appointment for their best-known senior ship's officer; wealthy passengers often displayed loyalty to a particular captain and none garnered a following like Captain Smith. Having him skipper the ship across the Atlantic would be the icing on the cake and maximise

the publicity and prestige surrounding the voyage. Smith was an able mariner and had enjoyed a long career absent of any significant examples of calamity. As such, his confidence is easily understood and only in hindsight does it appear misplaced. He was known to have offered the following thoughts on the safety of ocean navigation: 'When anyone asks me how I can best describe my experience in nearly forty years at sea, I merely say, uneventful. Of course there have been winter gales, and storms and fog and the like. But in all my experience, I have never been in any accident… or any sort worth speaking about. I have seen but one vessel in distress in all my years at sea. I never saw a wreck and never have been wrecked nor was I ever in any predicament that threatened to end in disaster of any sort. You see, I am not very good material for a story.' And, speaking of a former command, the *Adriatic*, he said: 'I cannot imagine any condition which would cause a ship to founder. I cannot conceive of any vital disaster happening to this vessel. Modern ship building has gone beyond that.'

The embodiment of luxury afloat
Titanic*'s unique selling points*

First class cabin aboard Titanic

The accommodation aboard *Titanic* was designed to exceed in standard all other passenger ships in service, including her sister-ship *Olympic*. Ismay was convinced that the way to achieve domination of the lucrative transatlantic trade was to give his shareholders and passengers something to gasp in awe at, from the lowliest emigrant family to the loftiest millionaire. The White Star Line was clear in its primary target market: the wealthiest sectors of European and North American society. That they succeeded in capturing the attention of these people is evident in the roll-call of the rich and famous booked onto the great ship's maiden voyage.

MORGAN'S NEAR MISS
Railroad tycoon and international financier John Pierpont Morgan was the man behind the conglomerate which controlled White Star – the IMMC. He intended to join the **Titanic** *for its maiden voyage – indeed, he had his own private suite and promenade deck booked – but fell ill and cancelled his passage 24 hours before departure. Having escaped a possible death on*

*the **Titanic** he nevertheless went on to die shortly after in 1913. Lord Pirrie was also due to sail but cancelled thanks to ill health.*

Granted, passenger liners were the only viable means of crossing the Atlantic before the jet age, but *Titanic* was different to all its competitors, especially for First class passengers with money to spend. She was bigger, more spacious, more luxurious, better styled, more exclusive than anything before – including her predecessor sister ship, the *Olympic*, launched on 20 October 1910. Between *Titanic*'s launch in May 1911 and her own maiden voyage eleven months later, Ismay co-ordinated a programme of fitting-out of quite extraordinary quality. The truly ground-breaking aspect to this was that it was not just First class passengers who benefited – the accommodation and facilities for Second- and Third-class travellers far exceeded anything they had known before too, equivalent to First- and Second-class standards in other ships, not least in the provision of good food at mealtimes and sleeping quarters. Ismay decided that with a bit

of rejigging, 28 lavish new staterooms could be created on the *Titanic* featuring wide and tall windows instead of more mean portholes. Other internal changes meant that *Titanic* would have the space to carry over 160 more passengers than *Olympic*. White Star's other key market was the emigrant trade.

Who sailed on the *Titanic*?
And where did they come from?

Passengers fell into three classes aboard most liners of the day. First class tended to play host to the wealthiest industrialists, aristocrats, socialites, senior military officers, bankers, professional athletes and so on. Accordingly, among those taking passage in First class on *Titanic* were some of the most prominent members of American society: millionaire real-estate owner Colonel John Jacob Astor IV and his 18-year-old second wife Madeleine; Isidor Straus, owner of Macy's department store in New York, and his wife Ida; tramway millionaire George Widener, who would give a dinner for Captain Smith on the fateful evening of 14 April; industrialist Benjamin Guggenheim; Pennsylvania Railroad executive John Thayer; millionairess Margaret 'The Unsinkable Molly' Brown; President Taft's military aide Major Archibald Butt; and American silent movie actress Dorothy Gibson. British First class passengers included Olympic-standard fencer and landowner Sir Cosmo and his wife, international fashion couturier Lady Lucy Duff-Gordon; and prominent publisher, editor and reformer William T Stead. Most privileged passengers brought with them their valets, servants, maids and even chauffeurs.

The price of First class tickets varied enormously. The average price of a ticket for a First class cabin for one was £30, approximately £2,200 today. For only the very wealthiest and perhaps most ostentatious, a private parlour suite – complete with its own promenade deck – cost £870, about £64,000 today!

Second class travellers were more of the respectable middle echelons of society: teachers, doctors, clergymen, lawyers, journalists. Most of the tourist families aboard ship also travelled Second class. The average ticket price

for an adult in Second class was £13, nearly £1000 in modern money and about what you might expect to pay to cross the Atlantic today on the *Queen Mary 2*, the only true transatlantic liner operating.

Third class – otherwise known as steerage – was home to the least wealthy passengers, usually emigrants moving to the United States from Britain, Ireland and Scandinavia. Like in the other classes, ticket prices varied, ranging from £3 (about £220) for a child's ticket, to between £7 (£514) and £9 (£660) for an adult depending on port of departure. The ticket price usually included rail

Lady Duff-Gordon, 1919

transport to one of the three ports of departure. Most Third class passengers were part of a family group; many women in Third class travelled with young children – often with their husbands having gone on ahead to set up a new life in America. Then there was widower Mrs Margaret Rice who was travelling from Ireland with her five excited young sons. Tragically, all six were to be lost within days.

WIPED OUT

Tragically, several other large families – including the Sages, a family of 11 emigrating from Peterborough to Florida; the Goodwins, a family of eight, emigrating from Fulham to New York; and the Anderssons, a Swedish family of seven emigrating to Winnipeg – perished in their entirety, their bodies among the hardest to identify for lack of surviving relatives.

Most passengers were British or American, particularly so in First and Second class. Other countries represented across the three classes included France, Germany, Uruguay, Argentina, Armenia, Bosnia, Russia, Croatia, Lebanon, Canada, Spain, Norway, the Netherlands and Japan. Overall, 33 nationalities were represented. A glance at the lists indicates about 120 Irish, 63 Finns, 26 Swedes and 24 Belgians, most of whom were emigrants travelling in Third class. Only twenty of the Finns survived, and just four Belgians. Two lucky Belgians were refused permission to embark at Southampton, and were turned away.

Interestingly, *Titanic* also carried 29 First and Second class passengers taking passage on just the 'cross-Channel' leg between Southampton and Cherbourg or Queenstown. One can only imagine the relief they must have felt on the morning of 16 April 1912 when news broke across the world. There were 13 honeymooning couples aboard ship. Sadly for many of them it was a guaranteed once-in-a-lifetime-only experience.

How many?
And in what class?

The number of passengers and crew embarked, by class and category, was as follows:

FIRST CLASS
Sailed:

Men	173
Women and children	156
Total	329

SECOND CLASS
Sailed:

Men	157
Women and children	128
Total	285

THIRD CLASS
Sailed:

Men	486
Women and children	224
Total	710

CREW
Sailed:

Men:	876
Women:	23
Total:	899

TOTAL	2,223

Proud point of departure
Southampton for the first and last time

The *Titanic*'s home port was Southampton, at that time the biggest liner terminus in Britain. The White Star Line had moved its transatlantic service there from Liverpool in 1907; the huge White Star dock was built to accommodate the company and was the base from which White Star's thrice-weekly transatlantic service was operated. At the turn of the 20th century the port boasted the world's biggest dry dock facilities, and was the principal port of embarkation for the men and materiel heading to South Africa during the Boer Wars (and again for the Normandy invasion in June 1944). Southampton's complex of large new dock facilities enabled it to handle the comings and goings of the biggest vessels of the day at all states of tide – a unique attribute.

While the *Titanic* underwent her sea trials off Belfast, the city of Southampton looked forward eagerly to her arrival on the south coast.

Titanic *at Southampton*

Four-fifths of all *Titanic* crew hailed from Southampton and all except a skeleton crew already aboard were waiting to embark. A piece in the *Southampton Daily Echo* – headlined 'The Coming of the *Titanic*' – spoke for the civic pride attached to the event: '... there is a special significance in the coming of the *Titanic* for it sets the seal once again upon the future of Southampton ... the race is on ... to keep up-to-date ... and the coming of the *Titanic* is a spur, if it is necessary, to our public men not only to keep the port their sacred trust, up to present needs, but a little ahead of them.'

Upon arrival in Southampton,

Titanic lay alongside and early next morning of 4 April the long task of coaling and provisioning the ship for the transatlantic voyage began. Due to a coal strike at the time, other ships such as *Oceanic* and *Adriatic* in Southampton docks had to be raided for their coal, 6,000 tons being needed. This threw many of their schedules out, and meant that several passengers were swapped onto the *Titanic* which was White Star's obvious priority. Many tons of provisions were brought aboard and stored, along with 560 tons of general cargo. Captain Smith and most of his officers boarded on the evening of 9 April. Meanwhile, most of the ship's crew had been recruited on 6 April and on 10 April, the day of sailing, they embarked at 7.30 a.m. to track down their working stations and living quarters. Half an hour later the last lifeboat drill took place. All was signed off as satisfactory.

A LIFE ON THE OCEAN WAGE
The range of crew wages aboard **Titanic:**
Captain Edward Smith:

£105 per month
Chief Radio Operator Jack Phillips:
£4 and 5 shillings per voyage
Assistant Radio Operator Harold
Bride: £2 and 2 shillings per voyage
Lookout George Hogg:
£5 and 5 shillings per month
Seaman Edward Buley:
£5 per month
Steward Sidney Daniels:
£3 and 15 shillings per month
Stewardess Annie Robinson:
£3 and 10 shillings per month

On the morning of the 10th, a large number of Second and Third class passengers arrived at Southampton railway station at 9.30 a.m. aboard one of the specially-run 'boat trains' originating from London Waterloo. They were transferred directly onto the ship for the midday departure. By 11 a.m. they were aboard, before the First class passengers' allotted embarkation time of 11.30 a.m. Similarly, Paris's Gare Saint-Lazare operated a boat train to Cherbourg for the passengers departing from that port later that evening.

Biscuit and grog of the highest quality
Provisioning the world's most luxurious ship

To feed and water over two thousand people three times a day for six days at sea required quite phenomenal quantities of stores and victuals combined with precise logistical management and expert timing on the part of the chefs, cooks, stewards and waiters right up and down the 'food chain'. The chief cook, Mr Charles Proctor, had a truly titanic shopping list to fulfil before the ship left port. The stores taken on to meet his projected catering requirements included a good variety offering choice and quality: beef, lamb and veal; chicken, turkey, pheasant, quail and plover; fresh fruit and vegetables; a ton and a half of tea and coffee; and 16,000 bottles of wine and beer. In addition, the ship got through 16,000 gallons of fresh water a day. In the event, much of the food and drink ended up 'in the drink'.
Food:
Potatoes 80,000 lbs
Fresh meat 75,000 lbs

Poultry and game 25,000 lbs
Fresh fish 11,000 lbs
Rice and pulses 10,000 lbs
Sugar 10,000 lbs
Cereals 10,000 lbs
Flour 250 barrels
Bacon and hams 7,500 lbs
Butter 6,000 lbs
Salted and dried fish 4,000 lbs
Tomatoes 3,500 lbs
Onions 3,500 lbs
Sausages 2,500 lbs
Peas 2,500 lbs
Coffee 2,200 lbs
Ice cream 1,750 lbs
Jam and marmalade 1,100 lbs
Grapes 1,000 lbs
Tea 800 lbs
Eggs 40,000
Apples 36,000
Oranges 36,000
Lemons 16,000
Grapefruit 13,000
Lettuce 7,000
Asparagus 800 bundles
Fresh milk 1,500 gallons
Condensed milk 600 gallons
Cream 300 gallons
Drink:
Beers 15,000 bottles
Wines 1,000 bottles

Spirits 850 bottles
Minerals and sodas 1,200 bottles

TABLEWARE AND LINENS

To ensure the highest levels of passenger comfort and convenience, Titanic's serving staff had on board a phenomenal amount of tableware and linen, to be used across the facilities in all three classes. They would have been expected to be able to know the differences between the individual types, too – especially when it came to serving in the First class dining rooms

Tableware:
Crockery 57,600 pieces
Cutlery 44,000 pieces
Glassware 29,000 pieces
Dinner plates 12,000
Ice cream plates 5,500
Tea cups 3,000
Wine glasses 2,000
Cruet 2,000 pieces
Egg spoons 2,000
Grape scissors 1,500
Soufflé dishes 1,500
Pudding dishes 1,200
Finger bowls 1,000
Oyster forks 1,000
Asparagus tongs 400

Nutcrackers 300
Linen:
Napkin 45,000
Towels 25,000
Sheets, single 15,000
Pillow cases 15,000
Bath towels 7,500
Blankets 7,500
Table cloths 6,000
Aprons 4,000
Bed covers 3,600
Sheets, double 3,000
Quilts, eiderdown 800

A room of one's own
Accommodation aboard Titanic

Whether you had a little or a lot of money, the facilities available aboard were incredible. After boarding, passengers would head straight for their cabins where their luggage would be waiting for them. There were 67 staterooms and suites for First class. The higher-spec suites came with two bedrooms, sitting room and private bathroom. Two of the best suites also came with their own 50-foot private promenade deck space. The opulent interior decoration varied from room to room and ran the gamut of fashionable and traditional designs, spanning Elizabethan, Louis XVI, Early Dutch, English Regency and more modern tastes. Rooms featured ornate furniture and plush carpeting.

Second class passengers enjoyed the use of spacious high quality private cabins complete with tasteful sycamore panelling. Third class passengers were accommodated according to situation. Families were berthed in their own cabins, while singletons on the cheapest fares were

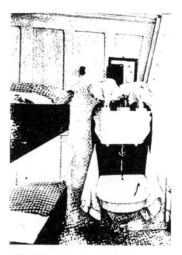

Third class cabin aboard Titanic

put into shared cabins rather than dormitories, separated per gender at each end of the ship. Women were accommodated in two to six-bed cabins; men could be in a room with up to nine others. All beds were equipped with mattresses, blankets and pillows, and all rooms were fitted with electric lightbulbs and heaters as standard. Not long ago, Third class passengers had been expected to bring their own bedding with them so *Titanic* offered a real improvement.

When it came to ablutions, sea water was used for sanitary purposes but fresh water was available for hand and dish washing. Only First class passengers had hot and cold running water on demand in the private bathrooms in their cabins. Second and Third class made do with reservoirs of water in their washstands. Two bathtubs were available for use. Fresh filtered drinking water was available to all.

First class passengers could make use of three electrically powered lifts to get between decks. For the first time anywhere, Second class travellers had access to another lift to themselves. Each of the four lifts had its own operator. Third class

passengers had to walk everywhere. Dotted about the ship were 48 remotely-kept clocks each showing ship's time. At noon on 10 April, as a band played 'Rule Britannia' ashore, *Titanic* was guided out into Southampton Water by six powerful tugs, narrowly avoiding colliding with the American liner SS *New York*, a near-miss which delayed the departure by an hour. Even with the delay, seven members of the ship's engineering crew turned up too late. Attempting a 'pierhead jump', they were refused permission to embark. Unperturbed, the *Titanic* headed out for her 24-mile hop across the Channel to Cherbourg.

The points of no return
Getting on at Cherbourg and Queenstown

The Paris boat train arrived at Cherbourg's maritime terminal at 4 p.m. on 10 April. Luggage was disgorged, collected and ferried to the quay where the two White Star tenders *Nomadic* and *Traffic* lay moored. *Nomadic*'s job was to take First and Second class passengers out to the *Titanic* which, due to her size, would need to anchor out in the harbour. *Traffic* was to transport the Third class passengers and

SS Nomadic

luggage. The tenders were boarded at 5.30 p.m. in expectation of the big ship's arrival, but she was late by an hour because of her near collision with the liner *New York* while leaving Southampton. Once alongside, *Traffic* took off 22 cross-Channel passengers and threw aboard the luggage, mail in bags and other provisions. *Nomadic* then brought out 274 additional passengers to add to the *Titanic* roll. Within twenty minutes all were aboard and as a band ashore played 'La Marseillaise' the *Titanic* turned and left Cherbourg at approximately 8.10 p.m.

Having sailed from Cherbourg with a fresh batch of new passengers including John Jacob Astor IV and Margaret Brown, *Titanic* arrived off Queenstown (now Cobh) near Cork on the southern Irish coast at 11.30 a.m. on 11 April 1912. Too big to come close inshore alongside any quay, *Titanic* anchored two miles out in the roads at Roches Point, where she would have been visible to the last set of passengers waiting on the dedicated White Star pier (which still exists, albeit in a dilapidated state) to board the bespoke tenders *America* and *Ireland* whose job, like *Nomadic* and *Traffic*, was to ferry passengers, cargo and mail out to the waiting liner. Seven passengers got off at Queenstown, rumoured to include one crew member wishing to desert. Nearly 1,400 sacks of mail were loaded aboard.

Of new First class passengers there were three; seven were for Second class and 113 mainly Irish

LUCKY BREAKDOWN
On his way to Cherbourg to catch his ship home, American Frank Carlson's car broke down and he missed the sailing.

emigrants for Third class, many of whom would have used Ireland's extensive rail network to arrive at the port. Of these 123 additional passengers only 44 would survive. At 1.30 p.m. the *Titanic* signalled her readiness to depart, the tenders got out of the way and the White Star's finest – carrying 900 tons of baggage, 2,223 people and the hopes and dreams of many poor emigrants with it – slipped her anchor for the last time, got under way to the tune of an Irish lament and steered west on the Great Circle Route towards the Nantucket lightship off the coast of Massachusetts. The Irish coastline receded into invisibility at about dusk. Those aboard busied themselves with the prospect of six days on the finest vessel ever built.

Unusual ways of boarding
Stories of stowaways and kidnappings

Were there stowaways? Possibly, as stowaways were a persistent problem for shipping companies despite tough measures being enacted.

The nature of a stowaway means that it is unlikely anyone who survived the sinking would have admitted to being one. Certainly no survivors did so, nor admitted to any knowledge of anyone else being a stowaway. But there is the intriguing evidence of fireman George Kemish who in 1955 wrote to Walter Lord to assist his research for the book *A Night to Remember*. 'There were also some stowaways that went down with the ship. Stowing away in those days was quite easy; it was very easy to walk ashore in New York. Restrictions then were not nearly so strict as now... "Jumping the freight" was another simple matter. No one knew who the stowaways

Orphans from the Titanic

were. Apparently they had no relations or friends. That type is to be seen in most big ports. Never missing, because they are never known – just world wanderers.'

If there were any aboard – and there is no documentary evidence to say for definite either way – they may have died in the sinking, in which case we will never know for sure.

Meanwhile, travelling incognito in Second class was a French family headed by Michel Navratil, a Slovakian-born tailor. Navratil had kidnapped his two young sons, Michel Jr. and Edmond, and bolted from his estranged Italian wife after taking the kids over the Easter holiday. After a brief stay in Monte Carlo, Navratil came to England and embarked under the alias Louis M. Hoffman, planning to emigrate with his boys to the United States. Navratil would die in the disaster but his boys survived in collapsible lifeboat D. Hauled aboard the rescue ship *Carpathia* in mail sacks, the boys could speak no English and could not make their identity known. Soon after, photographs of 'The *Titanic* Orphans' were published around the world in the hope that a

family member could identify them. Eventually their mother tracked them down and brought them back from New York on the *Oceanic*. Michel Jr was the last male survivor of the *Titanic*, dying in 2001 at the age of 92.

Rearranging the deckchairs...
Pastimes aboard ship

For the first four days aboard ship, all was revelry and pleasant routine. The ship was performing as billed, and the crew went about their business in a polished, discreet way. The social whirl continued unabated; children played on deck; friendships were made and renewed.

For active types on a First class ticket, there was a squash court down on F deck, the world's first shipborne heated saltwater swimming pool situated on the same deck, and an airy gymnasium on the starboard side complete with cycling and rowing machines.

GENTLEMEN'S LEISURE
First-class passenger Colonel Archibald Gracie – a retired US Army officer and real-estate developer

The gym aboard Titanic

in New York, and one of the best-known survivors of the disaster – later recalled that he enjoyed himself, 'as if I were on a summer palace by the seashore surrounded by every comfort. I was up early before breakfast and met the professional racquet player in a half hour's warming up preparatory for a swim in the six foot deep tank of saltwater heated to a refreshing temperature.'

Alternatively, one could stroll around the promenade decks as long as one wished, meeting and exchanging pleasantries with fellow passengers of old or new acquaintance, before reclining in one of the many deckchairs tucked out of the wind in sun-traps. After their exertions passengers could luxuriate in a fully equipped Turkish bath and steam room. And if this was not enough to iron out any pulled muscles or other ailments, the ship had its own infirmary and operating room manned by two physicians. *Titanic* even had its own onboard darkroom for the use of photography enthusiasts.

For the lazier passenger inclined to play cards, read or smoke, there were ample facilities: First and Second class smoking rooms (strictly for men only), First and Second class libraries and writing rooms for lady passengers. If you required a haircut ahead of

Archibald Gracie

dinner at the captain's table you could visit either of the two barber shops which boasted automated shampooing and drying appliances.

For Second class passengers, travelling on the *Titanic* was like going First class on other liners. They had the benefit of their own private smoking room, library and promenade deck, upon which deck games like shuffleboard and quoits could be played.

Third class passengers were provided with a piano in their saloon common room which saw much use. Games, cards, chess, minor gambling, singing and dancing were all popular pastimes for the steerage passengers. For men wishing to escape the clamour there was a peaceful Third class smoking room. The poop deck was open to Third class passengers for fresh air, a stroll and ball games. Meanwhile, their children were free to explore the many nooks and crannies around the ship.

White Star was keen that emigrants be impressed by the facilities offered in steerage, so that they would write to family and friends back home and recommend the service. And

who knows, thought J Bruce Ismay, one day an enterprising Third class passenger might just come back as a First class passenger.

Fit to bust
What's for dinner? And where?

The routine of the days at sea was one of incessant leisure, punctuated only by meal times. There was an enormous amount of ritual attached to these parts of the day, even to the extent that to announce that dinner was served, a bugler walked the decks sounding 'The Roast Beef of Old England'. The quantity and quality of meals varied from one class to the next. The meals you took aboard were dictated largely by the type of ticket you had purchased. First class had privileged access to three dining rooms set aside from the rest of the passengers; the main à la carte restaurant room on D deck was furnished in the Jacobean style, with a single height ceiling replacing the more traditional but less efficient triple-deck-height space of yesteryear. It was a large room: at over 10,000 square feet in area, it could seat 554 diners. The two other rooms were home to the open-all-day Veranda Cafe – complete with real palm trees, bright arched windows and wicker furniture – and the more informal, trendy Café Parisien, staffed by French waiters. This was popular with the younger set and located on the starboard side of B deck. These exclusive dining rooms were managed and staffed not by the White Star Line's own restaurant staff but by effectively a floating franchise of the Ritz Hotel. *Titanic* sported a refrigeration plant which provided

Menu from the Titanic

cold storage for the umpteen bars, pantries and water coolers around the ship.

Before dinner, First class folk usually assembled in the First class lounge for an aperitif. This was modelled on the Palace of Versailles and featured expansive fireplaces with statuary. To get to dinner, passengers might have used the famous Grand Staircase, perhaps the most emblematic feature of *Titanic's* fine fittings. Lit by an ornate skylight it featured a clock flanked by two figurines representing Honour and Glory.

First class passengers enjoyed sumptuous meals of the highest standards, as this blood-pressure-challenging dinner menu from 14 April testifies: oysters; consomme Olga; cream of barley; salmon, mousseline sauce, cucumber; filet mignons Lili; saute of chicken, Lyonnaise; vegetable marrow Farcie; lamb, mint sauce; roast duckling, apple sauce; sirloin of beef; chateau potatoes; green peas; creamed carrots; boiled rice; parmentier and boiled new potatoes; punch romaine; roast squab and cress; cold asparagus vinaigrette; pate de foie gras; celery; Waldorf pudding; peaches in chartreuse jelly; chocolate and vanilla eclairs; French ice cream.

LIFE ON THE OCEAN WAVE

One world record-breaking sale at an auction of Titanic *memorabilia was of a letter written on three sides of onboard stationery by First class passenger Adolphe Saafeld as the* Titanic *steamed towards Cherbourg, which offers a superbly detailed peek into the sumptuous conditions and leisurely pastimes experienced by the privileged passengers aboard* Titanic. *The item sold for £56,000 in April 2010.*

'After leaving at noon we had quite a little excitement, as the tremendous suction of our steamer made all the hawsers of the S.S. New York *snap as we passed her and she drifted on to our boat, a collision being averted by our stopping & our tugs coming to the rescue of the* New York. *You will probably have read of the occurrence in the papers.*

The weather is calm and fine, the sky overcast. There are only 370 First Class passengers. So far the boat does not move and goes very steadily. It is not nice to travel alone and leave you behind. I think you will have to come next time.

I have quite an appetite for luncheon. Soup, fillet of plaice, a loin chop with cauliflower and fried potatoes, Apple Manhattan and Rocquefort cheese, washed down with a large Spaten beer iced, so you can see I am not faring badly.

10pm. I had a long promenade and a doze for an hour up to 5 o'clock. The band played in the afternoon for tea, but I savour a cafe in the Verandah cafe with bread and butter and quite thought I should have to pay but anything and everything in the eating line is gratis.

At 6 o'clock we anchor outside Cherbourg and two tugs with passengers came alongside. Owing to our little mishap at Southampton we were all one hour late and had dinner only at 7.30 instead of 7 o'clock as usual.

The name of my friend, the White Star manager in London works wonders and I have a small table for two to myself. I made a very good dinner and had two cigars

*in the smoke room and shall
now go to bed as I am tired. But
for a slight vibration, you would
not know that you are at sea.'*

Second class passengers ate in their
own dining room, situated aft down
on D deck. Second class passengers
naturally did not enjoy quite so
sumptuous a choice of cuisine as First
class diners. However, their food was
prepared in the same modern and
superbly-equipped galley on D deck
which served the First class diners,
so the standard was still high. Their
dinner menu for the fateful night
of 14 April included, for starters:
consommé, tapioca, baked haddock
with sharp sauce; main course offered
a choice of curried chicken and rice,
spring lamb with mint sauce, and
roast turkey with cranberry sauce, all
accompanied with a choice of peas,
turnips, rice and potatoes; for dessert,
one could tuck into plum pudding,
wine jelly, coconut sandwich,
American ice cream, and assorted
fruit and nuts; all followed by cheese
and biscuits and coffee.

On many other liners the Third
class passengers were expected to
bring all their own food aboard.
Not on the *Titanic*, which offered
much better facilities for steerage
passengers including two of their
own dining rooms with meals
cooked for two sittings by Third class
kitchen staff. Instead of the usual
benches, *Titanic*'s poorest passengers
sat on chairs around neat covered
tables. Food provided was simple
but nutritious and wholesome,
and served in good quantities.

THIRD CLASS MENU,
14 APRIL
*Steerage passengers enjoyed the
following choice of food served on 14
April 1912. For many it would be the
last thing they ate:
Breakfast – Oatmeal porridge and
milk; smoked herrings and jacket
potatoes; ham and eggs; fresh bread
and butter; marmalade; Swedish
bread; tea and coffee.
Dinner – soup; fresh bread; cabin
biscuits; roast beef, brown gravy;
sweet corn, boiled potatoes; plum
pudding with sweet sauce; fruit.
Tea – cold meat; cheese;
pickles; fresh bread and butter;
stewed figs and rice; tea.*

Morse, Marconi and messaging
The value of wireless aboard ship

The first Marconi wireless sets to be installed aboard liners were those of the Norddeutscher Lloyd's *Kaiser Wilhelm der Grosse* and Cunard's *Lucania* in 1900. Wireless sets were a huge leap forward in bringing to an end the almost total isolation of vessels crossing large bodies of water such as the Atlantic. Conceived primarily as an aid to safe navigation, wireless aboard ship brought with it a new function: that of a ship to shore messaging service for paying passengers. Technically, official signals would be given absolute primacy at all times, but quite soon the majority of the time the shipborne Marconi office spent sending and receiving Morse would be on behalf of private customers who wished to keep in touch with business or social interests ashore. The telegram office was staffed by employees of Marconi, not the White Star Line.

LINES ARE OPEN
The fee to send a wireless telegram from the **Titanic** *was 12s 6d (twelve shillings and six old pence) for the first ten words, and 9d for every word following. Over 250 passenger telegrams were sent and received during the voyage.*

Early wireless sets suffered from low power and possessed only a short-range capability to transmit Morse code. As long as a receiving ship was within about 40 to 50 miles of the sending ship, signals could be relayed across open sea back to shore. Commercially available sets with the power to transmit across whole oceans – such as Guglielmo Marconi had demonstrated at the end of 1901 when he received his first transatlantic message in Newfoundland from Cornwall – were not widely employed until the late 1910s. Thus, in 1912, when the *Carpathia* wished to send news of her rescue of some of *Titanic*'s survivors, she had to rely on the message being relayed by the wireless operators aboard *Titanic*'s sister ship, the *Olympic*, whose set was much more powerful and thus able to transmit back to receivers in New York.

Flags and call-signs
How Titanic *identified herself at sea*

The use and display of flags at sea is an intricate art with many rules. In accordance with maritime custom, on her foremast *Titanic* flew the flag of her country of destination, in this case the Stars and Stripes of the USA. At the peak of her mainmast flew the red burgee or house flag of the White Star Line, which was a red, tapering, swallow-tailed pennant bearing a white five-pointed star. On the flagstaff at the stern flew a Blue Ensign until sunset when in port. At sea and within the sight of land or passing traffic the ensign would have been flown from the mainmast gaff. It was blue – instead of red, which is the standard for British commercial vessels – because *Titanic's* skipper, Captain Smith, was a member of the Royal Naval Reserve, which entitled him to fly a blue.

It is unlikely that the blue ensign was flying as the ship went down, since it would not be correct to display it out to sea, and certainly no point at night. It is presumed that the flag went down with the ship, secure in the flag locker. The Royal Mail's flag would also have flown from the foremast or foreyard, signifying that the ship was bearing British mail and in doing so could be called the 'Royal Mail Ship' RMS *Titanic* instead of plain old 'Steam Ship' SS *Titanic*.

TITANIC'S CALL-SIGN
Titanic*'s wireless call-sign was changed from MUC to MGY in early 1912 as the former was discovered already to have been assigned to another ship by the American Marconi organisation. For visual signalling the ship was assigned the four-letter code HVMP. If this needed to be displayed using flags, the following were hoisted vertically one above the other on the forward halyard (a line used to haul things aloft aboard ship):*
  Left half red/right half white rectangle
  Red saltire on white background
  White saltire on blue background
  White rectangle with blue inner border of one third radius
  The code to denote passengers' wireless messages was ADVISELUM.

You have been warned
Ice warnings received –
and ignored?

Over the first four days of her voyage, *Titanic's* wireless operators received from numerous other ships many warnings of ice ahead along her route. Ice was an occupational hazard for transatlantic liners heading for North America, but recent conditions in Greenland and the north-east Canadian coast had created an unusually large amount of ice which drifted further south than usual. Captain Smith was not overly concerned. But in fact the *Titanic's* route – the summer 'Southern track' – was not southern enough this year.

On the 11th she received word from six ships stopped in or passing through heavy ice ahead; on the 12th,

five more; the 13th, three; and on the 14th, seven more. These messages were logged in the wireless record and passed to the bridge for the attention of the ship's officers.

Sunday 14th was a clear, crisp day, rather more chilly than the previous days. *Titanic's* wireless set had broken down the day before and as the vessel came into range of the station at Cape Race on the south-eastern tip of Newfoundland the two Marconi operators were coming under increasing pressure as passengers realised they could make contact with the outside world again. A backlog of messages gathered; at the same time, ice warnings started to roll in, each bringing a little more fidelity to the location and possible extent of the ice in *Titanic's* way.

ISMAY AND THE ICE
So what of Ismay's reaction to the ice warnings? One of those received on Sunday 14 April came via the nearby steamer **Baltic** *at 1.42 p.m. It was handed by Captain Smith to Ismay just before Ismay went down for lunch. Normal procedure was to post the ice warning in the chart room*

for the use of the navigating officers.
Instead Ismay put the telegram in his
pocket and promptly forgot about it
for five hours until he was asked for
it by Smith just after 7 p.m. **Titanic**
received other warnings later that
day; one was received at 7.30 p.m.
but Smith never saw it as he was
at a dinner hosted by the Wideners.
He excused himself at around 9 p.m.
and returned to the bridge where
he discussed the weather conditions
with Second Officer Lightoller, and
left instructions to be contacted if the
situation became doubtful.

During the day, the temperature
readings had been falling. The *Titanic*
was due to alter her course in the
late afternoon of the 14th when
she would arrive at 'The Corner',
a point on the route where liners
changed heading towards New York.
Captain Smith decided to delay his
turn by 25 miles in order to get
further south and avoid the reported
ice. Meanwhile, the sea and air was
getting colder – by 7.30 p.m. it was
down to 3.9 degrees Celsius. The ice
was only 50 miles away now.

Up in the crow's nest as dusk turned

to a clear, calm and starry night, the
lookouts were warned to keep their
eyes alert to ice. During the evening
Titanic upped her speed by half a knot
to over 21.5 knots; Ismay and Smith
knew they had coal in hand and four
days into the voyage she was lighter
than when she left port, so they could
afford to light up any spare boilers.

It has been debated whether by
speeding up slightly Smith wanted to
make up for his detour designed to
get round the ice, or whether Ismay
wanted to beat *Olympic*'s maiden
voyage timings. At the subsequent
inquiries, Ismay denied telling
Smith to increase *Titanic*'s speed. Of
course, Smith was no longer around
to question. But crossing as fast as
possible was a goal which every self-
respecting transatlantic captain would
already have had in mind; on her
second passage to New York – when
Smith was aboard – the *Olympic* had
managed to arrive a day early. To
cross the Atlantic as fast as a new ship
could steam was part of the challenge
enjoyed by shipmasters of the big
lines, particularly ones cut from the
same kind of cloth as Captain Smith.

At 9.40 p.m., with the temperature

down to zero degrees Celsius, a wireless message was received from the *Mesaba* not far away: 'Ice report in latitude 42°N to 41°-25'N longitude 49° to 50°-30'W. Saw much heavy pack-ice and great number large icebergs; also field ice. Weather good; clear.' Wireless operator Jack Phillips took down the message. According to some, it never reached the bridge as his fellow operator Harold Bride was getting some much needed sleep and Phillips, busy transmitting the backlog of commercial messages accrued that day, put it to one side. Others contend that the bridge received the message but, trusting that ice would be seen in good time, never acted on the contents. Either way, this was the last ice warning received via wireless. On the basis of several reports after the accident, it was estimated that the ice field *Titanic* was already beginning to steam through – so far without a scratch – was 120 km long, lying on a northeast-southwest axis, and 20 km wide.

By 11 p.m. *Titanic* had closed on the position of the Leyland Line's *Californian*, lying stopped, blocked by ice in temperatures below freezing.

Phillips was busy getting through to Cape Race at long range; the signal was faint and he had a lot of traffic to work through. So when *Californian*'s wireless operator tried to contact the *Titanic* through the ether with the warning 'I say, old man, we're stopped and surrounded by ice', the clumsy interruption combined with the strength of the close-range signal was too much for Phillips' tired ears and he snapped back: 'Shut up. Shut up. I am working Cape Race.' If the *Californian* had prefaced its message with the correct call-signs it may have been listened to as official traffic, but

Jack George Phillips

unfortunately Phillips was not in the mood to give anyone the benefit of the doubt. The *Californian*'s operator, himself exhausted after a long day working on his own, switched off his set after a further 30 minutes spent trying to reach *Titanic* – the only ship in range of his wireless set – and retired for the evening. As a result, Phillips noted neither the message nor the import of *Californian*'s position at the time.

'Ice, right ahead'
Up in the crow's nest with the lookouts

On the night of April 14, the sea was very calm and still. At 11:40 p.m. the two lookouts sat in the crow's nest and strained their eyes against the biting cold wind blowing right into their faces. Lookout Frederick Fleet and his fellow lookout, Reginald Lee, had taken over the crow's nest watch at 10 p.m., relieving George Symons and Archie Jewel. Symons would later testify that he could tell ice was in the offing – not only was it perishing cold aloft but he could smell the ice around.

Settling down for the watch, Fleet is thought to have complained about the lack of binoculars. Fleet's eyesight had not been tested in five years; Lee's in thirteen. By now *Titanic* was moving through the water at nearly 40 feet per second. Suddenly Lookout Fleet sighted an iceberg immediately ahead of the ship, about half a mile away in the gloom; he rang the crow's nest bell three times and reached for the nearby telephone that connected the nest to the bridge.

He told them, 'Iceberg, right ahead.' He was courteously thanked for the information. Then the duty officer ordered the ship hard to port and rang down to the engine room to stop engines (not put them in reverse, which would have slowed the way of the ship and impaired her turning ability accordingly). Over the next 37 seconds or so, the *Titanic* slowly reacted to the calm but hurried orders and, to the lookouts, it seemed in the last couple of seconds that she would pass safely to port of the iceberg. But she didn't quite – over the course of 10 seconds the iceberg scraped and bumped along the starboard side of the ship, shearing off rivets and buckling plates along an approximately 300-foot section, before receding into the night behind them as the helm was neatly swung back to starboard to ensure *Titanic*'s stern didn't follow suit. The engine room reacted to the final command to Stop Engines.

LOOKOUT FREDERICK FLEET

Born in Liverpool in 1887 and brought up in a series of foster homes, Fleet first worked at sea as a deck boy in 1903, working his way up to Able Seaman. He took a job as a lookout on the White Star liner **Oceanic** *and stayed for four years before joining the* **Titanic** *for her maiden voyage. After sighting the iceberg and giving his report to the bridge, Fleet remained at his post for a further 20 minutes, by which time the* **Titanic** *had come to a stop. Back down on deck, as the chain of command began to react to the evidence of unsustainable damage, Fleet assisted in the loading of lifeboats, including Lifeboat 6, which he then got away in along with Archie Jewel. After being picked up by* **Carpathia**, *Fleet*

was quickly posted to the **Olympic**, *but, feeling disgusted with the White Star Line, which he allegedly thought looked upon former* **Titanic** *crew as an embarrassing reminder of the company's errors, he left White Star in favour of other lines. Working on the sea until 1936, he got a job with Harland and Wolff, and later became the shore Master-at-Arms for the Union-Castle line. In later years he was a familiar face in Southampton, where he sold newspapers on the street. Fleet's wife died at the end of 1964 and Fleet found himself homeless. Sadly, he committed suicide by hanging himself in early 1965. He was said to have suffered from*

feelings of guilt about his survival, and doubts about whether he could have seen the iceberg sooner. He was buried in a pauper's grave in Southampton.

The gash that was actually a buckle
What's the real damage?

Many passengers and crew barely perceived the collision, and if they did they were for the most part unaware of the attendant damage and unconcerned. In any case, wasn't this ship known to be unsinkable? Indeed, some passengers went on deck and kicked about chunks of ice in a playful manner. For others, particularly those lower down in the bowels of the ship or along the starboard side, forward – the impact was very much more audible and tangible ('as though someone had drawn a giant finger along the side of the boat', according to Lady Duff-Gordon) and its effects immediately obvious. Captain Smith, occupied in his chart room, immediately returned to the bridge and sought the advice of his duty officers. Thomas Andrews

was sent for, and Ismay arrived soon after.

FEET WET
Among the first passengers to notice something was not right were Third class men David Buckley and Carl Johnson. Woken in their bunks they got out to investigate and found water – already up to ankle height – invading their cabin.

It has been argued that the *Titanic* might have suffered less critical damage had she hit the iceberg head-on, because any damage would likely have been confined to fewer compartments (though those in the first 100 feet of the ship would have been severely crumpled) and the ship could have run aboard the iceberg, thereby remaining afloat. But the ship's officers on the bridge and on the helm reacted to the situation according to the rules of seamanship in which they had been schooled, and deliberately steering a brand-new 45,000 ton ship at 21.5 knots towards an iceberg looming out of the mid-Atlantic was not one of the generally accepted rules.

In contrast to popular perception, recent studies tend to suggest that instead of tearing a continuous gash along 300 feet of the starboard hull, the steel plate hull was buckled under the impact in sections. Based on survivor's accounts it has been possible for researchers using computer software to calculate the area of openings created in the hull through which the sea could enter. One study gave the following figures (in square metres) per compartment breached, aft from the bow:

Fore peak	0.056
Cargo hold No.1	0.139
Cargo hold No. 2	0.288
Cargo hold No. 3	0.307
Boiler room No. 6	0.260
Boiler room No. 5	0.121
Total area	1.171

This is higher than an original estimate of 1.115 square metres made by Harland and Wolff staff, but not by much. The upshot was that the resulting influx of water from these openings in the hull eventually overwhelmed the pumps.

INUNDATED

One estimate says that 4,000 cubic feet of water entered the ship in the first ten minutes. An hour after the collision **Titanic** *had taken on 24,000 cubic feet of water.*

As the pressure inside the ship and outside began to equalise, over the first hour after the collision the rate of flooding steadily decreased from a maximum of about 400 tons per minute. In the second hour, the flooding inside *Titanic* almost reached a balance point, but as the bow began to grow heavier and heavier it dragged more and more non-watertight decks and openings under the water, causing a renewed onslaught of flooding which overwhelmed the internal subdivision bulkhead by bulkhead, compartment by compartment, aft from the bow. As chief designer Thomas

Andrews noted to the captain, the ship was irreversibly on its way down now.

The chief designer of the *Titanic*, Thomas Andrews
There at the beginning, there at the end

A talented draughtsman and nephew of William Pirrie, Harland and Wolff's main owner, Thomas Andrews was managing director and head of the plans department at the company's yard in Belfast. It was common practice for shipbuilders to put men aboard a ship for her maiden in-service voyage, just in case anything needed attention. Having spent years on her design and construction, naturally it was Andrews's right and privilege to represent Harland and Wolff's 'Guarantee Group' and accompany his creation across the Atlantic, as he had with the *Adriatic*, *Oceanic* and *Olympic*. Thus he did so along with an eight-man group of skilled workers. Berthed as a First class passenger in cabin A-36 on a complimentary ticket, his last letter to his wife Helen shows a man proud of the fruits of his draughtsmanship: 'The *Titanic* is now about complete and will I think do the old Firm credit tomorrow when we sail.'

After dinner and back in his cabin on the night of 14 April, Andrews was sat poring over his ship's blueprints in an effort to solve some minor niggles when the ship ran into the iceberg. Andrews barely noticed the impact but he was swiftly summoned to the bridge by Captain Smith. Soon after, he made off with Smith to make an inspection of the damage. At first they noticed a strange list developing; then they stopped to stare at the water already rising in the squash court (32 feet above the waterline) and mail rooms. Returning to the bridge, they quietly consulted and after a few calculations Andrews passed on the dreadful news that the 'unsinkable' ship was indeed going down at the head – the extent of the damage was simply too much for the ship to bear – and would likely do so in about 2 hours. His calculations were correct.

Like many of his fellow men in authority, he spent the next hour or so encouraging the donning of lifebelts and helping passengers into lifeboats. He was last seen by a ship's steward by the fireplace in the First class smoking room, staring into space near a painting of Plymouth Harbour, his lifebelt discarded on a table nearby. A popular man, the 39-year-old ship designer's body was not recovered.

Bad tidings
The men in the mail room

L ike other White Star Line vessels, as well as those of the American Line, *Titanic* was licensed by a 1905 joint agreement between Britain and the US to carry mail between her ports of call. As a result she was entitled to sail as a 'Royal Mail Ship'. It was an important commercial service for the postal services of both countries, and a reliable source of income for the line. Three thousand mail bags were loaded at Southampton with more being hauled aboard from tenders at Cherbourg and Queenstown. Five members of staff from the two postal services – two British (John Smith and James Williamson) and three

Americans (John March, William Gwinn and Oscar Woody, whose 44th and final birthday would be on 15 April 1912) – sorted the mail in the mail room aboard ship while she was under way, and were accommodated in Second class cabins. The mail room was located on G Deck. Soon after the collision with the iceberg, and while the postal staff worked busily to sort their valuable cargo, their exertions were permanently interrupted by sea water flooding into the mail room. Immediately they set about trying to shift the mail sacks and scattered parcels out of the mail room and up a level to F Deck. Unfortunately their efforts were in vain – all the mail was lost as the lowest decks were swiftly submerged, and all five men lost their lives. Only March and Woody's bodies were ever found. March was buried at sea, and Woody ashore in New Jersey. Mail tickets and other paraphernalia were found in his pockets. No mail has yet been recovered from the wreck site on the sea floor. It's possible that none survives intact.

Binoculars and searchlights
Would they have made a difference?

On 10 April 1912 the *Titanic* had set out for Cherbourg. On this first leg the lookouts up in the crow's nest complained that they lacked binoculars. They had had them on the trip down from Belfast to Southampton earlier in the month, but now they were nowhere to be seen. Where had they gone? The explanation is Second Officer David Blair, who had since left the ship when he was replaced by Lightoller in a crew reshuffle. The binoculars were still onboard but remained locked away in what had been Blair's cabin. Debate would rage after the disaster as to whether the lack of binoculars played a significant part in the ship hitting the iceberg. Surely having binoculars would have allowed the

lookouts to spot the danger earlier? Certainly Lookout Frederick Fleet testified that he would have found them useful.

While it's true that the lookouts did not use any binoculars on the night of 14 April, it was not common practice to use them to keep a general lookout. This was done with the naked eye. Binoculars would then be used from the bridge if watchmen stationed aloft spotted something of particular interest. At night – particularly on moonless nights like the 14th – binoculars are generally of little use. Icebergs were usually detected in the dark by observing the white spray of waves against the ice. It being a relatively still night and flat sea, the lookouts had a job on their hands. Binoculars probably wouldn't have helped a great deal.

Similarly, many critics have remarked on the lack of a searchlight fitted to the *Titanic* to assist with night-time navigation. Surely if she had been equipped with a powerful light the lookouts would have spotted any icebergs in the path of the vessel as she raced along at over 21 knots? Opinion is divided.

The lookouts relied on their eyesight at night to detect any objects in the water. Had a light been used it would have disrupted their carefully attuned night vision. In that case you would need the beam – even a powerful light illuminates little in open sea – to score and retain a lucky hit on the iceberg, which is no sure thing. Chances are the fatal iceberg would be completely overlooked, though a light might have helped prove the general proximity of the ship to an ice field. But if the captain really wanted to preserve the safety of the ship and its passengers, the speed of his ship in waters where the presence of ice had been confirmed ought to have been his priority. A slower ship means more time for lookouts to detect and react to inbound objects along the ship's course. A light would probably not have helped at 21.5 knots.

That iceberg
Where is it now?

A man named Stephan Rehorek took what may well be the only genuine photograph of the most notorious iceberg in human history (admittedly the list is short) six days after it was hit by the *Titanic*. Thought to be a Czech seaman aboard a German steamer of the Norddeutscher Lloyd line, the *Bremen*, which was en route to New York when it passed close to the scene of the tragedy, Rehorek decided to take photographs of the two biggest icebergs still in the vicinity. When he landed in New York, Rehorek wrote a postcard home describing the awful scene around the wreck site – bodies and wreckage still floated about, along with the two icebergs. He promised to send photos of the icebergs and, several weeks later, had postcards made out of them which he sent home from Cherbourg. And so these images may have disappeared into history were it not for the fact that they were discovered in 2000 by a German

Titanic *iceberg?*

journalist and *Titanic* fan, Henning Pfeifer. Immediately the possible significance of the postcards became clear to Pfeifer. He said: 'As soon as I looked at this one iceberg I knew I was holding a piece of history in my hand. I remembered reading evidence from the inquiry after the disaster when one survivor had described the iceberg as looking like the Rock of Gibraltar but a mirrored version. This iceberg was just like it but it had a fresh break on one side.'

How plausible was Rehorek's belief and Pfeifer's assertion? Of course, there is no way to be certain. But in coming to the conclusion that he was looking at the frozen culprit, Pfeifer considered the location of the *Bremen* and the iceberg at the time of the photo, the likely speed and direction of drift and current, and survivors' accounts of the appearance of the berg compared to the photos taken by Rehorek. According to Pfeifer, the clincher is the 'fresh break' on one side of the iceberg, along with a noticeable overhang and distinctive outline which tallies with eyewitness reports. The original print currently resides in a bank vault in Munich.

HOW BIG WAS IT?

Eyewitness accounts of the size of the iceberg above water range from 50 to 100 feet high and 200 to 400 feet long, with a corresponding estimate of about 500 feet below the surface. Lookout Fred Fleet thought its height was somewhere between the forecastle head and the crow's nest (approximately 50 feet and 90 feet respectively). No-one will ever know the absolute truth. These dimensions equate to an object that has been estimated at anywhere between 100,000 to 300,000 tons in weight. Probably only ten per cent of the bulk of the iceberg was visible above the surface of the sea. On a moonless night an object that size out in the pitch dark would have been extremely difficult to pick up visually, even if it was a white iceberg. Given that the Titanic *was the brightest thing on the surface of the sea for dozens of miles around, the job of keeping an effective lookout has been compared to driving down an unlit motorway at 70mph with no headlights or road markings but with all your car's interior lights switched on!*

As the berg headed south from its origins in probably Greenland's glacier fields it will have slowly begun to melt. Melting icebergs eventually find that their centres of gravity shift, resulting in the iceberg constantly being in a state of turning over on itself. Opinion is divided over whether the iceberg was in warm enough water for that process to have begun, and accounts varied regarding the colour of the iceberg as the ship passed by, but one intriguing theory holds that sighting the iceberg could have been even more difficult thanks to the darker blue underwater ice being exposed in the night air as the mountain of ice turned over.

In any case, the iceberg partially responsible for the deaths of over 1500 people probably melted into the sea in a matter of weeks. An interesting aside, next time you're pouring yourself a whisky on the rocks: it's a mathematical probability that the

whisky and the ice contain a few molecules of the iceberg that sank the **Titanic***. Ironically, you'd have to hack some ice from another iceberg to avoid your ice cubes containing* **Titanic** *water. Why? The iceberg would have formed from snow falling long before the* **Titanic***'s eventual nemesis melted back into the global water cycle.*

CQD or SOS?
Titanic*'s distress calls*

Forty-seven minutes after the collision, and once the damage done to the ship had been thoroughly assessed as serious, at 12.27 p.m. the wireless operators aboard ship went to work sending out emergency distress calls over the radio. The signal they used was 'CQD', which in Morse code is dash-dot-dash-dot, dash-dash-dot-dash, dash-dot-dot. This

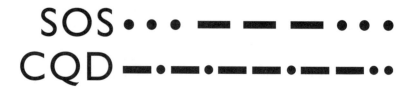

was a Marconi standard procedure to be used by all Marconi wireless sets (which, in practice, meant the vast majority of wireless sets in use anywhere). Originally the signal, created for land telegraphs, comprised only CQ – short for 'all stations attend' – but Marconi thought that this did not impart enough urgency; so for serious emergency calls he added the letter D for 'distress' to make CQD. It did not mean to stand for 'Come Quick, Danger' or 'Come Quick, Distress'; the CQ was more likely based on the French 'sécu' of 'sécurité'.

How did this differ from SOS, which is much more familiar today? SOS started out life in 1906 after an international telegraphic convention decided on a new standard signal. The German delegation proposed SOE which was their standard signal of enquiry, but the final 'E' is just a single dot in Morse and it was felt that this risked getting lost in the transmission or receipt. Instead a second 'S' was added to SO to make 'SOS', which has the much more easily remembered Morse pattern of dot-dot-dot, dash-dash-dash, dot-dot-

dot. Contrary to popular belief it was not devised to stand for 'Save Our Souls' or 'Save Our Ship'.

On the night of the disaster, the operators used both CQD and SOS. *Titanic* was not the first ship ever to have used SOS but it was not commonly used outside of German lines so she may have been among the first British vessels to have used it. Harold Bride joked to Jack Phillips that they ought to use it as this might be the only time they got a chance to do so. Using a mixture did not create confusion as is sometimes claimed. On the other hand, a failure to grasp the seriousness of the *Titanic's* condition probably did lead to confusion among those receiving the distress calls. The furthest away to receive it was *Olympic*, some 500 miles distant, which continued to misunderstand until 1.15 a.m., believing her sister was afloat and underway. Other vessels to hear the calls were the *Baltic* (243 miles), *Virginian* (170 miles), *Frankfort* (153 miles), *Birma* (70 miles), *Carpathia* (58 miles) and *Mount Temple* (49 miles).

'CQD OLD MAN'

The Marconi operators aboard ship were in frequent communication with their fellow operators aboard other ships including the **Carpathia** *and, 400 miles away, the land station at Cape Race, Newfoundland, manned by Robert Hunston, Jack Goodwin and Walter Gray. The most famous of the signals received by wireless operator Harold Cottam on the* **Carpathia** *was this, sent by Jack Phillips aboard* **Titanic** *at 00:35: 'CQD CQD SOS SOS CQD SOS. Come at once. We have struck a berg. CQDOM [It's a CQD old man]. Position 41.46 N., 50.14 W. CQD SOS.' The* **Carpathia** *got the message, acknowledged, and worked up steam for a direct high-speed course.*

Harold
Bride

At around the time *Titanic* started issuing distress calls, the first lifeboat was loaded and lowered, and Quartermaster Rowe arrived on the bridge clutching the ship's rockets. Captain Smith ordered him to fire one every five minutes. In the glare of the first rocket's explosion, the passengers gathering on the deck in their lifebelts became less reluctant to leave ship. Rockets meant the ship was in serious trouble.

About 10 miles away, the *Californian* still lay, unaware of what had happened to the *Titanic*. Third officer Charles Groves, earlier spotting some lights on the horizon, had tried to signal the unknown ship (*Titanic*) but had failed to work the Morse set properly. Now, *Californian*'s Second officer Herbert Stone noticed the rockets. Yet his vessel had still not picked up a distress call from *Titanic*. *Titanic* continued to fire rockets but they did not explode high enough and failed to draw attention from *Californian*. In the *Titanic*'s wireless room, Phillips looked at his colleague Bride and said, 'I think we're in a tight pickle.' Bride replied, 'You think we'll be having sand for breakfast?'

They continued to send increasingly desperate distress calls.

The show must go on
The Titanic's *stoic musicians*

One of the most enduring human images of the *Titanic* disaster is that of the ship's musicians bravely refusing to put down their instruments and abandon their position on the boat deck as the ship went down at the head. It seems that the legend is actually true in this case – while passengers of all classes were scrambling to abandon ship, the musicians are widely reported by survivors to have continued playing right up until the last moments, if not quite with the water lapping around their highly polished shoes and with the deck planking rapidly becoming a wall. Remarkably, it seems they took the decision to remain out of a sense of duty as well as a devotion to their art. They must have known that their fates were sealed.

There were eight musicians employed on the *Titanic's* maiden voyage when she left Queenstown on 11 April 1912: Wallace Hartley (bandmaster, violin), Roger Bricoux (cello), Theodore Brailey (piano), John Woodward (cello), John Clarke (string bass, viola), John Hume (violin), Percy Taylor (piano) and Georges Alexandré Krins (violin). Each was a renowned professional musician at the top of his game, experienced in playing aboard transatlantic liners. Four nights later not one of them was still alive.

They were accommodated in a large shared cabin in Second Class. Before 1912 musicians were usually taken on directly by the shipping companies and enjoyed reasonable rates of pay, union protection and status as members of crew. But now, employed by a Liverpool-based talent agency, CW & FN Black, things were less rosy for men in their position. The agency had secured an exclusive contract with the shipping lines – so in order to work, musicians were more or less forced to deal with Black's, which meant accepting lower pay and demotion of status from crew to passenger, including the cessation of a uniform allowance.

The eight men were hired as two orchestras – a trio and a quintet. The trio – consisting of a pianist, cellist

The band aboard Titanic

and violinist – performed melodies of a distinctly French style in the Café Parisien and the reception area outside the à la carte restaurant; the quintet played background music in the First class lounges and reception areas and gave after-dinner concerts. The White Star Line songbook comprised 350 tunes ranging from trendy ragtime to rousing hymns and stylish waltzes, guaranteeing variety and novelty to any passenger who cared to listen.

CREW OR PASSENGERS?

After the disaster, when the task of tallying up the dead occupied the authorities, there was some confusion over whether to classify the ship's musicians as crew or passengers. Impetus to seek definition on the matter was increased when it was discovered that the musicians were not covered by any insurance policy. They did not pay a fare like a passenger, but neither were they directly employed by the shipping line. Over the course of a lengthy debate in a stream of letters between the British Board of Trade and the Registrar General of Shipping and Seamen, the figures were adjusted and recalculated at least twice. In the end it was decided that the musicians should be thought of as passengers rather than crew, so their fatality statistics are registered among the official figures for deceased passengers. For insurance purposes the White Star Line maintained that the men were employed by the Black agency and therefore covered by them. The Black agency maintained that since the men were classed as passengers, they fell under White Star's responsibility. In January 1913 a third status was conferred on the dead musicians by the **Titanic Relief Fund,** *which announced that it would treat the eight as members of the crew and make assistance payments to their survivors as a result.*

Signalling to the end
The scene in the wireless room

The wireless set-up was housed on the boat deck along the centreline of the ship. (It had been moved inboard from the previous outboard location on *Olympic*, to give up the valuable window space to paying passengers.) It consisted of three rooms – a noisy transmitting room, a quiet receiving room, and a bedroom with bunks for the operators. The operators were Marconi employees and wore uniforms distinguishing them as such, complete with Marconi logos on the buttons, sleeves and caps. They took their meals together with the Royal Mail employees in a dining room on C deck.

Jack Phillips was only 22 and yet

he was already the senior wireless operator aboard ship. On the night of Sunday 14 April he was exhausted after a long shift spent repairing a damaged transformer in their set and clearing the resulting backlog of messages. He was about to call it a day when the collision occurred. Shortly after, Captain Smith arrived in the wireless room and gave orders to radio out for help. Phillips stayed at his post, sending out both CQD and SOS signals as instructed. Harold Bride, his fellow Marconi operator, was sent to and from the bridge to apprise the captain of any updates from the *Carpathia* which had been contacted and was now closing at full speed. As the full desperation of the situation became apparent, and as more and more lifeboats left the sinking ship, Smith arrived in the wireless room to relieve the Marconi men from their duties. He told them, 'Men, you have done your full duty. You can do no more... That's the way of it this time.'

Their dedication to searching the airwaves in the hope of salvation for the *Titanic*'s passengers and crew was staunch. The last wireless messages emanating from their set were timed at 2.17 a.m., just three minutes before *Titanic* took the plunge. Phillips was prevented from carrying on when the generators gave up, thereby ceasing the supply of electrical power to the wireless room as well as the lights which had hitherto burned brightly. All was darkness and confusion now. Phillips had to fight to get his lifebelt back from a man who had stolen it. Bride went forward to assist with the launching of collapsible B, the last lifeboat aboard ship. As the ship went down, Phillips leapt into the sea and found himself clinging onto the side of the upturned collapsible. Bride was there too, as was Lightoller. They spoke in hope of the vessels which might come to their rescue. Phillips weakened and by morning he was dead. His body was not recovered.

HAROLD BRIDE'S EYEWITNESS ACCOUNT
Harold Bride was the junior wireless operator aboard **Titanic**. *Assisting some male passengers to launch the final collapsible boat from the tilting deck, it was struck by a large wave and Bride was washed overboard still clinging to the now upturned boat. As he reported to the* **New York Times** *a few days after being rescued: 'The next I knew I was in the boat. But that was not all. I was in the boat, and the boat was upside-down, and I was under it. And I remember realizing I was wet through and that whatever happened I must not breathe, for I was under water. I knew I had to fight for it, and I did. How I got out from under the boat I do not know but I felt a breath of air at last. There were men all around me – hundreds of them. The sea was dotted with them, all depending on their lifebelts. I felt I simply had to get away from the ship. She was a beautiful sight then. Smoke and sparks were rushing out of her funnel. There must have been an explosion, but we heard none. We only saw the big stream of sparks. The ship was turning gradually on her nose – just like a duck that goes for a dive. I had only one thing on my mind – to get away from the suction. The band was still playing. I guess all of them went down. They were playing 'Autumn' then. I swam with all my might. I suppose I was 150 feet away when*

the **Titanic**, *on her nose, with her after-quarter sticking straight up in the air, began to settle – slowly.'*

Make that the last verse...
The musicians' last hurrah

Within half an hour of the *Titanic* lurching past the iceberg that struck the fatal blow, all eight musicians had mustered in the First class lounge on A Deck. They began to play upbeat melodies at 12:15 a.m.; their repertoire included the 1911 ragtime tune 'Oh, You Beautiful Doll' and the up-tempo Irving Berlin number 'Alexander's Ragtime Band', a scene portrayed in James Cameron's *Titanic* (1997). None were wearing life-belts; all wore their usual band uniforms.

STUPID LETTER OF THE WEEK
Before the cruel month of April 1912 was even over, the family of lost violinist John Hume received a bill from the Black agency demanding that payment be forwarded to cover

his unpaid uniform expenses. It can only be hoped that this was the product of grinding administrative process and nothing more deliberately insensitive.

It is commonly suggested that the band played to still the nerves of the anxious passengers; was it an excessively British response to put up such pretence of normality in such dire straits? If so, was there any dissent among the band? None is recorded. Early on, it is possible that the full scale of the ship's impending peril was not apparent for some time to come. In any case, as the night of crisis wore on, the band periodically removed itself higher up out of the way of the flood rising through the lower decks, stationing themselves on the Grand Staircase at the level of the boat deck. Most passengers were already at the lifeboat stations or making preparations to meet their makers when the band took up their final position in the open night air on the forward part of the exterior boat deck.

The band is reputed to have turned towards more patriotic numbers as the tension rose. National anthems and popular rallying tunes such as 'The Star-Spangled Banner' and Londonderry airs featured as alarm grew into panic and disorder. With the writing on the wall, a religious tone set in with hymns and reverential songs such as 'Abide With Me' and 'Eternal Father, Strong To Save'.

Debate still rages over what piece was being played in the last moments before the music was drowned out. Survivors' accounts vary wildly, but a definite preponderance of accounts refer to two or three particular possibilities. Favourite among them is the hymn 'Nearer My God to Thee', which was reported by British and American passengers alike. Confusion enters the frame when it is noted that the hymn is sung to markedly different tunes in those countries. Nevertheless, both nationalities of passenger reported hearing it, and bandleader Wallace Hartley was reputed by former bandmates to have said he would play it if he was ever on a sinking ship. Other accounts name the waltz 'Autumn' by Archibald Joyce as the very final tune. The truth can never be fully established. The

musicians' bravery, though, has never been questioned.

'Be British, boys, be British!'
The last words and deeds of Captain Smith

How did *Titanic*'s captain die? We know he died at the scene and that his body was never recovered. But according to eyewitness statements, Smith met his death in at least three different ways. Most credible is the account which says Smith waited calmly on the bridge, having returned there to go down with his ship after walking the decks for one last time, releasing his crew from their duties at approximately 2.17 a.m. A variation states that he was swept overboard from the bridge by a wave, and was last seen swimming back to the bridge to be in position for the final plunge. Another account states that Smith was last seen striking out for a lifeboat, which he evidently never boarded. A fourth offers the explanation that Smith committed suicide by shooting himself in the head with a pistol. And what about his last words? Survivors claimed to have heard him utter the immortal line to his officers and crew in earshot: 'Be British boys, be British!' This is probably press speculation. One account says that having dragged a child through the water to a waiting boat, he refused to be hauled aboard himself, stating 'Goodbye boys, I'm going to follow the ship!' It's possible that as Smith walked the decks, his final words in command of the ship were simply 'It's every man for himself'. In the confusion and tumult, no clear and irrefutable evidence remains.

'A queer feeling'
The unsettled chief officer, Henry Wilde

The second in command aboard ship after Captain Smith was the Executive or Chief Officer, 39-year-old Henry Tingle Wilde of Merseyside. Well known and trusted by Smith as an expert on the *Olympic*, Wilde was transferred across for the *Titanic*'s maiden voyage at Smith's request, necessitating a reshuffle of the rest of *Titanic*'s officers. This resulted

in the lowest-ranking officer, Second Officer David Blair, being forced to drop off the bottom of the pecking order, taking with him knowledge of where the lookouts' binoculars were kept. Lucky for Blair (whose duties were taken up by former First, now Second, officer Lightoller), but not so lucky for Wilde.

Not so lucky either for Captain Herbert Haddock, recently given command of the *Olympic*. Haddock was the youngest captain in the White Star Line. He took the *Olympic* out for the first time in April 1912 without many of the ship's normal senior officers – Chief Officer Wilde,

Henry Wilde

Lord Pirrie and Bruce Ismay inspecting Titanic

First Officer William Murdoch, Chief Engineer Joseph Bell, Chief Surgeon William O'Loughlin and Chief Purser Herbert McElroy – who had been transferred over to *Titanic* to provide experienced staff for her maiden trip. Only a few months later he nearly ran the *Olympic* aground on rocks off Land's End. And Haddock was an experienced ship's master which just goes to show what beasts the *Olympic* class were. The very best seamanship was the very least needed to navigate them safely.

Wilde is known to have written a letter to his sister, dated 11 April 1912, in which he offered some unsettling thoughts about his new berth: '....I still don't like this ship, I just have a queer feeling about it...'

There is some mystery over Wilde's behaviour on the fateful night. At 6 p.m. on April 14th he was relieved by Lightoller after an uneventful watch during which the ship's speed had remained constant despite the earlier warning of ice. After the collision Wilde accompanied the captain and ship's designer Andrews on their inspection tour. He is then believed to have spent the remaining time directing the loading and lowering of boats on the port side (the even numbered boats). At one point he asked Lightoller where the ship's guns were kept. Lightoller led him, Captain Smith and First Officer Murdoch to the gun locker in the First Officer's cabin. Wilde was described as having a 'powerful look' as he shoved a Webley revolver and ammunition into Lightoller's hand, saying, 'Here you are, you may need it.' Back on deck, this time on the starboard side, Wilde assisted in launching a boat. When no more women or children were forthcoming, Wilde ordered the boat to be lowered, whereupon both White Star chairman Bruce Ismay and

William Carter – a First-class passenger – are alleged to have jumped in. Ismay, eternally shamed by his own survival, would later claim to have been bundled into the boat by Wilde but arguably this does not ring true given Wilde's staunch adherence to the principle of 'women and children first' demonstrated elsewhere on the boat deck.

ISMAY'S CONTROVERSIAL ESCAPE

At both the British and American inquiries Ismay was coy to the point of silence about the circumstances of his own escape into lifeboat C. His general line was that in the absence of any other passengers wishing to get in, he had taken the opportunity to board. Some time later he is alleged to have confessed to a family member that he had been ordered to board by Wilde for the reason that his subsequent testimony would be needed to deflect blame for the accident from Captain Smith's shoulders. In any case, Ismay was criticised widely for taking a seat when plenty of other men of his standing had stood back. He came under pressure by White Star to retire. His reputation never recovered despite the protestations of his supporters and he lived quietly in Ireland until he died in 1937.

Wilde then crossed over the deck to the port side to assist Lightoller who had come under a lot of pressure from crowds attempting to board a collapsible lifeboat. In desperation Lightoller was forced to draw his revolver and demand that a cordon be placed around the boat to control the surging crowd. Once order was restored Wilde ordered Lightoller to get aboard the collapsible but he refused and leapt out of it before it was lowered away. At this point, eyewitness accounts diverge. Some say that Wilde was last seen struggling to free two further collapsibles from the roof of the officers' house before the water got him. A contemporary obituary lauded him: 'He had been in the service of the White Star line for about fifteen years, and it was understood that he was shortly to be given the command of one of the Company's vessels. He was an officer of merit and deservedly popular, and those who knew him will be satisfied that at the time of trial and danger, he did his duty and died at his post in the spirit of the true British sailor.' At least two other survivors' accounts stated that Wilde actually shot himself. Either way he did not survive and his body was not recovered.

The evacuation under way
The scandal of the half-filled lifeboats

Titanic had twenty lifeboats in total. Early in the ship's fitting out, one of the managing directors at her builders had suggested using a new type of davit, which was larger and could handle more boats more quickly. Had this suggestion been followed up, the *Titanic* could have had capacity for 48 lifeboats, enough for every passenger and crewman aboard. But the White Star Line declined to spend the money on cluttering up their promenade decks, and they were quite within the law to do so: British Board of Trade regulations dating from 1894 stipulated a basic rule that all British ships over 10,000 tons must carry 16 lifeboats with a capacity of 5,500 cubic feet, plus sufficient floats and rafts for 75 per cent of the lifeboat capacity. In a ship of *Titanic's* size – 46,000 tons or so – these rules could guarantee lifeboat capacity to only a fraction of the ship's passengers and crew. The belief in *Titanic's* 'unsinkability' played a huge part too in the complacency. Despite the capacity being legal and above board – and by adding collapsible boats White Star was technically exceeding the statutory requirement – this did not stop members of the crew having private misgivings about what would actually happen should the need to abandon ship become real.

CONRAD'S CRITICISMS

In his article 'Some Reflections on the Loss of the **Titanic***' of 1912,* **Heart of Darkness** *author Joseph Conrad offered the following caricature of the august body whose outdated regulations helped create the conditions for a huge loss of life: '… if ever a loss at sea fell under the definition, in the terms of a bill of lading, of Act of God, this one does, in its magnitude, suddenness and severity; and in the chastening influence it should have on the self-confidence of mankind… the Board of Trade, which, having made the regulations for 10,000 ton ships, put its dear old bald head under its wing for ten years, took it out only to shelve an important report, and with a dreary murmur, "Unsinkable", put it back again, in the hope of not being disturbed for another ten years…'*

The complement of lifeboats comprised the following: fourteen 30-foot wooden whaler-type lifeboats, rated to take 65 people; two emergency cutters, each able to take 40 people; and four Englehardt collapsible canvas boats, each able to accommodate 47 people. Thus total lifeboat capacity was calculated at 1,178 people.

In the early hours of 15 April only 16 lifeboats were successfully launched, and those that did get away were often not filled to capacity. A theoretical 472 lifeboat spaces went unused as a result. There were 2,223 passengers and crew embarked on 14 April 1912. Thus just 52 per cent of all souls aboard could be accommodated in the ship's boats. The other half would have to take their chances with a lifebelt. *Titanic* carried 3,560 lifebelts and approximately 50 floats. But would more boats have made a crucial difference? It's argued that, in fact, the technology of the day did not offer a reliable system for loading, lowering and launching a large number of lifeboats in a short space of time. In tests conducted by the US inquiry, the whole process took on average 18 minutes per boat. It should not be forgotten that the *Titanic* actually sank in very benign conditions. She did not sink suddenly, or capsize, or get battered to death by heavy seas; she foundered in a calm sea, on an even keel, over the course of two and a half hours. But even under those circumstances only 16 out of 20 lifeboats were launched from their davits, and 'half-filled' in some cases. Contemporary critics of what they called the post-disaster 'absurd fetish of lifeboats for all' may have been right in the sense that additional lifeboats may have made no difference in alleviating the losses of the *Titanic*. There is little point in having dozens of extra lifeboats if they cannot be filled and launched by the crew before the ship is under water.

The first lifeboat to leave – Lifeboat 7, skippered by Lookout Hogg, which left at 12.45 a.m. – carried only 28 people out of a possible 65. The second to leave – Lifeboat 5 – carried 35 people. This is probably because passengers feared abandoning the biggest ship in the world for a comparatively flimsy wooden craft on the open Atlantic, especially as they did not appreciate the true danger they were in at that time. Captain Smith's orders that the lifeboats 'stand-to' in order to assist

those unable to board them were ignored; occupants feared the suction that a sinking ship can create, and feared their boats being swamped.

THE SHAME OF LIFEBOAT 1

Of all the lifeboats to leave undermanned, none stoked up more post-disaster anger and resentment than Lifeboat 1, which got away at 1 a.m. with a truly shameful 12 people aboard. Five of these were First class passengers, the remainder seven crew. Among them were both Lord and Lady Cosmo Duff-Gordon, travelling under the false name of Morgan, and their secretary. Very quickly after being rescued life became awkward for the Duff-Gordons, who were the target of much opprobrium on both sides of the Atlantic, especially after it was revealed that Cosmo had offered £5 to each bereft crewman in the boat so they could buy themselves new kit. This act, probably prompted at heart by compassion, backfired as all it did was raise suspicions that the Duff-Gordons had effectively 'bought' the acquiescence of the crew at the expense of other passengers. Their public image was not furthered when Lady Duff-Gordon insisted on mustering 'her' crewmen for a souvenir team photo on the quayside in New York, while in the background dead bodies of Third class passengers were transferred ashore from the **Carpathia.** *Three years later, Lady Duff-Gordon booked passage aboard the* **Lusitania** *on what turned out to be its last voyage, before cancelling her trip due to ill-health. The* **Lusitania** *was torpedoed by a German submarine on 7 May 1915. Lady Duff-Gordon's fashion empire imploded in 1934 and she died, broke, in 1935. Her husband had died four years earlier.*

All lifeboats contained men, despite the women and children first policy. Male crew were ordered into boats to operate them, and in many cases men were let aboard when no more women and children could be found before a lifeboat was ordered to clear away. Lifeboat 12, lowered at 1.25 a.m., came the closest to containing only women, with 20 mainly Second class women and two crewmen aboard, but it was still woefully under-filled. Lifeboat 15, lowered

at 1.35 a.m., was the most full, with 69 people aboard, mostly Third class passengers and crew.

Clearly there is a general trend discernible – the later the lifeboat left, the more full it tended to be. Nevertheless, at 2 a.m., there were still 1500 people on the decks of the *Titanic* with nowhere to go; the water was already up to the promenade deck.

'A MASS OF HUMANITY'

Striking out for the stern as the ship increasingly settled at the stem, one eyewitness recalled that 'there arose before us from the decks below a mass of humanity several lines deep converging on the Boat deck facing us and completely blocking our passage to the stern. There were women in the crowd as well as men and these seemed to be steerage passengers who had just come up from the decks below. Even among these people there was no hysterical cry, no evidence of panic. Oh the agony of it.'

Only two lifeboats returned to collect swimmers from the site. In doing so they plucked nine people out of the water. Three of these later died.

ABOARD COLLAPSIBLE B

Collapsible B was the last boat to leave the **Titanic** *as she sank at 2.20 a.m., under the command of Herbert Lightoller. Thirty men (including Archibald Gracie, Jack Thayer and Harold Bride) found themselves clinging to the upturned canvas boat which was in danger of sinking for most of the small hours until they were eventually rescued by other boats. Bride recollected: 'I was all done when a hand reached out from the boat and pulled me aboard. It was our same collapsible. The same crowd was on it. There was just room for me to roll on the edge. I lay there not caring what happened. Somebody sat on my legs. They were wedged in between slats and were being wrenched. I had not the heart left to ask the man to move. It was a terrible sight all around – men swimming and sinking.*

I lay where I was, letting the man wrench my feet out of shape. Others came near. Nobody gave them a hand. The bottom-up boat already had more men than it would hold, and it was sinking. At first the larger waves splashed over my clothing. Then they began to splash over my head, and I had to breathe when I could. As we floated around on our capsized boat and I kept straining my eyes for a ship's lights, somebody said, 'Don't the rest of you think we ought to pray?' The man who made the suggestion asked what the religion of the others was. Each man called out his religion. One was a Catholic, one a Methodist, one a Presbyterian. It was decided the most appropriate prayer for all was the Lord's Prayer. We spoke it over in chorus with the man who first suggested that we pray as the leader.'

Many men were turned away from the collapsible and other boats for fear of overloading whatever capacity and buoyancy remaining. Thayer remembered the unwillingness of a nearby boat to help them: 'The partly filled lifeboat standing by about 100 yards away never came back. Why on Earth they never came back is a mystery. How could any human being fail to heed those cries?'

Women, children...
And Americans first?

Research published in 2009 by the Queensland University of Technology suggested that the patterns of behaviour exhibited by British male passengers were a significant contributor to the likelihood of their death or survival aboard the *Titanic*. Behavioural economist David Savage claimed that during a life-or-death crisis the Edwardian-era British male was likely to adhere to ingrained social conventions based around class rules, cultural norms of behaviour and above all a notion of 'gentlemanliness'. Using the core concepts of supply versus demand – in this case the obvious factor being availability of places in lifeboats – the research sought to show whether these social norms held over time or were replaced by 'survival of the fittest' instincts, and how quickly. Was it possible to discern that his socially-demanded altruism had hamstrung the British male's chances of survival? Could his chances be compared to those of his perhaps less hidebound, more individualistic American brethren, for instance?

Mr Savage's research seemed to say it could: 'Proportionally more Americans survived than expected, which could be because British passengers followed social queuing etiquette which may not have been as strong in America. While the passengers in the first and second-class berths on the *Titanic* had a higher probability of survival it may be that they were closer to the lifeboat deck but also it was the norm that they received preferential treatment. We expect that first-class passengers had higher bargaining power and better access to information about the imminent danger, which may have increased survival rates. Overall, the results indicate a strong support that social norms and altruism do matter.'

According to the research, being a woman aboard the *Titanic* made you 52 per cent more likely to survive than a male. Being a woman with a child gave you a 70 per cent better chance of surviving.

THE BIRKENHEAD DRILL

The 'Birkenhead Drill' was the name given by Victorians to the doctrine of 'women and children first' in life-threatening situations. It sprang from the story of the British troopship HMS Birkenhead which sank with the loss of 450 men off South Africa in 1852. The available lifeboat was used to put the ship's 20 women and children in and the men were ordered to stand fast on deck. By 1860 the phrase 'women and children first', which has come to be so heavily associated with the Titanic disaster half a century later, had come into popular British parlance.

However, it is entirely unfair to point to American passengers as any less willing to assist in the evacuation of women and children than male passengers of any other origin. Very many moving anecdotes exist to testify to the bravery and chivalry of men of all nations, prominent among whom are Americans. One example was Colonel Gracie; reputed to be the last man aboard ship, his selfless actions saved several lives. Gracie died on 4 December 1912, aged 53 and 'haunted by his memories of the wreck of the *Titanic* and never completely recovered from the shock of his experiences... Gracie did nothing to banish the tragedy from his thoughts... The events of the night of the wreck were constantly on his mind... In his last hours the memories of the disaster did not leave him. Rather they crowded thicker, and he was heard to say: "We must get them into the boats. We must get them all into the boats."'

The wreck of the Birkenhead

Titanic's last hour
The giant slips under the waves

From the perspective of the lucky occupants of the lifeboats already launched, the liner was an impressive sight in her final moments. Her cabin and deck lights continued to glow, albeit at an increasing angle, reflected in the still waters, and from the boat deck music wafted through the air. The hubbub on deck was growing louder. Unseen below, Third class passengers still struggled to find ways to the surface; some were actively hindered by gates, manned or not; others were carefully led up by stewards.

HART IN THE RIGHT PLACE

John Edward Hart was a 31-year-old Londoner and former soldier who signed on as a Third class steward ten days before the disaster. He was also one of the stewards who organised and led groups of steerage passengers up to the boat deck. If you accept his testimony and the attendant timings and statistics – and not everyone does – Hart was a hero. He is credited with personally ensuring the safety of roughly half the total number of Third class women and children who survived.

Hart's quarters were down on E deck, next to the Third class dining room. Awakened by the collision, Hart and some of his colleagues got dressed and left the room to investigate. Soon, Chief Third class steward Kiernan arrived and gave instructions for the stewards to go and look after their passengers. Hart walked to where the 58 Third class passengers under his care were berthed, along E deck in sections K and M. Having woken his flock he assisted them in donning their lifebelts and led them into the passageway outside.

Shortly after, Hart received word to start passing the women and children

*up to the boat deck. He started off by
leading a first group of 30 through
the passageways, via C deck and the
aft well deck, forward into the First
class area and up onto the boat deck.
After safely loading his first group
into Lifeboat 8, Hart went back below
to fetch the remainder, along the way
passing two other third class stewards
shepherding their groups topside.
Once below Hart repeated his
journey until the rest of his
passengers had been safely delivered
onto the boat deck and into Lifeboat
15. Just as Hart was preparing to
head back down to collect yet more
passengers, a group of men started
to mob Lifeboat 15 in an effort to
get aboard. Hart was obliged to help
resist the desperate men, which he did
until he was ordered by First Officer
Murdoch to get into the boat to help
row it away. As a result, Hart lived to
be picked up by the* Carpathia. *He
would later be called as a witness at the
British inquiry in May 1912, at which
he testified that all the gates along
his evacuation route had been opened
already by the time he led his steerage
passengers to the boats. He was the
only one of eight Third class stewards*

*to survive the night. Where Kiernan's
orders were issued from is unclear, as he
did not survive the disaster.*

At 1.40 a.m. the last of the white
distress rockets was fired. At 1.55 a.m.
the last of the rigid lifeboats, Lifeboat
4, was launched from the port side.
She only needed to be lowered 15
feet to the water, instead of the usual
60 feet. Now the collapsibles C and
D were unlashed from their moorings
and connected to the rigid lifeboat
falls. By this time the forecastle and
everything forward of it was under
water. The bridge was only a few feet
from the waterline. Even so, lights still
burned thanks to the heroic efforts
of the engineers who remained
below decks. But at 2.10 a.m., as men
struggled to clear collapsible B into
the water, the ship's angle increased
as internal flooding took its final grip.
The band played on. As desperate,
panicked passengers tried to escape
the rising tide creeping up the deck,
the stern of the ship rose even higher
out of the air. The foremost funnel
fell forwards, killing swimmers in
the water. The wave generated by
the funnel swept collapsible B, lying

upturned on the surface, away from the ship. As the ship pivoted under the surface, her hull joints under unbearable strain, anything not screwed down began to shift inside the ship, creating a thunderous noise audible to everybody. The smallest china plate to the enormous boilers crashed forwards inside as the ship's stern rose almost to the perpendicular as room after room was swallowed by the surging sea. Passengers on deck fell or jumped into the sea as the lifeboats close by struggled to pull away. Finally, at 2.20 a.m., the entire ship slid under the waves, travelling at about 10 mph as she went. Fifteen hundred people were left shouting, screaming, crying out, praying and fighting for their lives in the frigid waters of the North Atlantic, seen or heard by 700 or so of their fellow travellers fortunate enough to have secured a seat in – or at least a grip on – a lifeboat. By 3.30 a.m. that cacophony had turned to deathly silence.

HARROWING SOUNDS

The most senior surviving officer from the **Titanic** *was Charles Herbert Lightoller: 'What I remember about*

that night – what I will remember as long as I live – is the people crying out to each other as the stern began to plunge down. I heard people crying, "I love you."' In the dark, many in the lifeboats listened to hundreds of invisible people dying around them, occasionally illuminated by flashes of torchlight. According to survivor Eva Hart, 'The sounds of people drowning are something that I can not describe to you, and neither can anyone else. It's the most dreadful sound and there is a terrible silence that follows it.' Survivors also remarked that they could hear the occasional wave breaking against ice dotted all around them in the darkness.

The Strauses
Together forever

Among the affluent First class travellers who perished was prominent Jewish businessman Isidor Straus, travelling back to his home in New York, accompanied by his wife Ida. Born in Bavaria, Germany, in 1845, Isidor had emigrated to the US in 1854 with his family, settling in Georgia where the Strauses established a dry-goods store. His wife, Rosalie Ida Straus (née Blun) was born in Worms, Germany, in 1849. Isidor was employed as a store clerk while gaining an education at a local college. In 1862, during the American Civil War, the family moved to Ohio and Isidor became involved in a company employed in blockade-running for the Confederate South. After the war Isidor and his brother Nathan moved to New York and took an interest in the company R. H. Macy & Co, founded in 1858. The Straus brothers secured agreements to sell china and other goods through Macy's store. Macy himself died in 1877 and ownership of the store passed

Isidor Straus, 1903

through the Macy family until in 1896 Straus acquired ownership of the firm which is still known today as one of New York's pre-eminent shops, famously sponsoring the Fourth of July fireworks parade and producing the Macy's Thanksgiving Day Parade. It bills itself as the world's largest store.

In early 1912 Isidor, Ida and their daughter Beatrice had steamed across to Europe on the German HAPAG liner *Amerika*. They favoured travel by German lines when possible. In hindsight, failure to adhere strictly to this policy cost the family dear. Returning from Southampton without their daughter, the Strauses paid £221 15s 7d for cabins C-55-57 on the *Titanic*. Travelling with them were Isidor's servant John Farthing and Ida's maid, Ellen Bird.

John Farthing died in the disaster, and his body, if recovered, was unfortunately never identified. Ellen Bird survived and went on to work for another *Titanic* survivor, Frederic Spedden, who had also been on the ship the Strauses took to get to Europe!

A WATERY END
Ironically, Frederic Spedden died of a heart attack in a Florida beach club swimming pool many years later.

Ida's steadfast refusal to leave her husband to face his death alone is famous. Mrs Straus almost entered Lifeboat 8 but changed her mind, turned back and rejoined her husband. Fellow passengers and friends failed to persuade her otherwise. She is reputed to have told Isidor: 'We have lived together for many years. Where you go, I go.' Mr and Mrs Straus – described as a 'sweet and gentle old couple... a real life Darby and Joan' – found a pair of deck chairs and sat down together

to await their fate with dignity. Both were engulfed by the freezing water as the ship plunged down. Ida's body was never recovered. The body of Mr Straus was later recovered by the *Mackay-Bennett*. Their joint memorial service was attended by a staggering 40,000 people.

You can't take it with you...
John Jacob Astor IV

Colonel John Jacob Astor IV, the inheritor of some 55 million dollars in 1892 (approximately 1.3 billion dollars today), was easily the richest man aboard ship, and thanks to his social prominence was a key personality of the day, often featuring in contemporary and more modern retellings of the *Titanic* story. Member of the Astor clan, whose rags-to-riches immigrant story – originally built on property development, opium and fur trading – bewitched the Eastern seaboard of America for generations, John Jacob was to many observers a simple and uncommitted jack of all trades – businessman, investor, slum landlord, inventor, author, philanthropist, part-time army officer, husband, father, philanderer and tourist.

In 1909 he divorced his first wife Ava Lowle Willing after 18 years of bitter and joyless marriage, during which rumours of adultery and immorality on both sides had abounded in the upper echelons of New York society. At the age of 47 in September 1911 he invited further scandal when he announced his intention to remarry, this time to an 18-year-old socialite named Madeleine Talmage Force (Astor's son and heir William Vincent Astor was a year her senior). Shunned somewhat cruelly by New York society, Astor decided to escape the gossip and immediately travelled to Europe and Egypt for a second honeymoon with his new bride. While overseas the new Mrs Astor fell pregnant and, insisting that their child be born in the United States, the couple cut short their tour. The last leg would be the crossing back to New York from France.

Embarking in Cherbourg on Wednesday 10 April, the Astors were accompanied by their valet, Victor Robbins; Madeleine's maid, Rosalie Bidois; and a nurse, Caroline Endres. Also in tow was their beloved Airedale terrier, Kitty, destined for a cosy kennel aboard the *Titanic*. Also joining the ship at Cherbourg would be Margaret Brown, a New York contemporary of the Astors, who would come to be semi-fictionalised later and known as 'The Unsinkable Molly Brown'.

Margaret Brown

'UNSINKABLE' MOLLY BROWN

One of the most memorable characters to endure from the **Titanic** *story is Molly Brown, usually portrayed as a doughty, privileged yet down-to-earth force to be reckoned with. But who was she and how did she get her nickname? Margaret Brown was a Missouri-born, Denver-made millionairess, socialite, suffrage activist and later resident of New York, married to a self-made mining tycoon James Brown (though they separated in 1909). Rescued from lifeboat number 6 – into which she had helped several of her fellow survivors, and which she helped to row away from the sinking liner – by the* **Carpathia,** *Margaret Brown was put ashore at New York harbour's Pier 54 where she and other survivors were met by a crowd of over 30,000 people thronging to hear of the historic tragedy. When reporters in the crowd asked her for an explanation of her survival – which famously included her strident wish to return her under-manned lifeboat, crewed by Quartermaster Robert Hitchens, to the scene to pick up more swimmers – she is alleged to have replied 'Typical Brown luck. We're unsinkable.' Thus was born the legend of the Unsinkable Molly Brown, cemented in the following decades by portrayals in films and books and even a fictionalised Broadway musical of 1960 with the same title. The real Margaret Brown went on to champion a host of good causes across America, was awarded the French* **Légion d'Honneur** *for her philanthropic services, and died in 1932 in New York. Her former home in Denver is now the Molly Brown House Museum.*

'Molly' had been one of the few not to cold-shoulder John Jacob and his bride back home; coincidentally she had also had cause to cut short her own travel plans due to family illness and return to New York from Europe at the same time. The Astor party boarded and enjoyed the best in transatlantic service that money could buy. They dined with the Captain and rubbed shoulders with an exclusive subset of the First class passengers.

Did Astor find himself in a First

class bar shortly after the liner struck the iceberg in the small hours of 14–15 April? Certainly one line ascribed to Astor has famously passed into legend – 'I asked for ice, but this is ridiculous' – but biographers seem of the opinion that this does not sound much like Astor, not noted for his sense of humour. Other probably far-fetched anecdotes still persist: that Astor made it his mission to release all the dogs from their kennels; that he helped disguise a young boy with a woman's hat to assist his escape.

What we do know from reliable records is that Astor went to his cabin and informed his wife that things were afoot. He helped to dress Madeleine and sought to reassure her of the worth of a life-belt by slashing open a spare one to expose its buoyant innards. When they reached A deck they were both wearing belts. Colonel Archibald Gracie, in the vicinity of Astor as he and his wife negotiated entry to Lifeboat 4, said that after helping Madeleine – along with her maid and nurse – into a boat, Astor asked the officer in charge, Second Officer Lightoller, if he could get in with

her, due to her 'delicate condition'. Lightoller refused, explaining that all women and children were to be accommodated first.

His wife recalled him saying, 'The sea is calm. You'll be all right. You're in good hands. I'll see you in the morning.' They then kissed goodbye and Astor stood at the rail, smiling down at his wife as her boat was lowered away. Madeleine thought she could see a dog scuttling along up and down the deck – was it Kitty? Meanwhile, Astor retreated dutifully, merely asking for the boat number before apparently turning away to help others into what became the last lifeboat to be launched.

Madeleine's boat moved away, and less than an hour later she watched as the *Titanic* slipped beneath the waves, taking one of the world's richest men – the father of her unborn child – with it. All the ladies in the lifeboat survived; Astor's valet Victor Robbins, and Kitty the dog, did not. Reports vary as to the manner of Astor's death – some say he was hit and killed by a falling funnel or flying debris during the ship's death plunge, others report he was drowned.

ASTOR'S BODY IS IDENTIFIED

The body of JJ Astor was picked up by the cable steamer **Mackay-Bennett** *on 22 April. His body was identified by the initials on the labels sewn into his fine clothing. A number of objects and effects were found about his corpse, helping to identify him further, as the official description shows:*

NO. 124 – MALE – ESTIMATED AGE 50 – LIGHT HAIR & MOUSTACHE.

CLOTHING – Blue serge suit; blue handkerchief with 'A.V.'; belt with gold buckle; brown boots with red rubber soles; brown flannel shirt; 'J.J.A.' on back of collar.

EFFECTS – Gold watch; cuff links, gold with diamond; diamond ring with three stones; £225 in English notes; $2440 in notes; £5 in gold; 7s. in silver; 5 ten franc pieces; gold pencil; pocketbook.

FIRST CLASS. NAME – J.J. ASTOR

From steerage to dressing Guggenheim
Bedroom steward Henry Etches

Henry Samuel Etches was a 41-year-old bedroom steward stationed with First class on the port aft side of B deck. He was responsible for tending to the needs of passengers in eight cabins on B deck and one on A deck, that occupied by Thomas Andrews: 'Every morning at 7 I went to his cabin. I would take him some fruit and tea. I used to see him again when he dressed at night. That would be a quarter or twenty minutes to 7, as a rule. He was rather late in dressing...' At the time of the collision Etches was off duty but he emerged from his berth and wandered forward along E deck to the Third class berths where he came upon a passenger handling a piece of ice. 'Will you believe it now?' he was asked.

Returning to his First class passengers, Etches helped them dress and put on their lifebelts. One of his wards was American millionaire mining tycoon Benjamin Guggenheim, one of the wealthiest men aboard ship, travelling with his valet and chauffeur. Guggenheim was reportedly only aboard the *Titanic* because an earlier passage booked for the *Lusitania* had changed and *Titanic* was the next fastest ship.

Etches eventually persuaded a reluctant Guggenheim to put on warm clothing, followed by his lifebelt, and directed him to the boat deck. As Etches worked his way down the row of cabins, he knocked on one and explained through the door what the trouble was. He was ignored, so he moved on up to the boat deck to take his chances. Etches was eventually rescued aboard Lifeboat 5.

Not so Guggenheim. Famously, he would later decide to return to his cabin in order to change into his smartest evening wear, along with his valet. He was later heard to remark, 'We've dressed up in our best and are prepared to go down like gentlemen.' He was last seen sauntering up the deck, lighting a cigar. The bodies of Guggenheim, his valet and his chauffeur were not recovered. According to the papers, one of Guggenheim's last acts was to leave a message for his wife: 'This is a man's game and I will play it to

the end... tell her that no woman was left on board this ship because Ben Guggenheim was a coward. Tell her that my last thoughts will be of her and our girls.'

This noble sentiment is somewhat spoiled when one learns that Guggenheim was also accompanied on board by his French mistress, singer Leontine Pauline ('Ninette') Aubart, who survived and immediately began to sue the White Star line for $25,000 for personal injury and a further $12,000 for lost luggage, including four trunks for hats, dresses and lingerie; a toilet-bag with silver fittings; 24 dresses; 9 hats; 24 pairs of shoes; 12 sets of knickers; 24 lace corsets; and 22,000 francs' worth of jewellery.

White Star faced lawsuits in excess of $16 million for loss of life and property. Successfully dodging the bullet for four years, aided by legal loopholes and limited liability status it finally agreed to pay out just $664,000, shared among the claimants from July 1916 onwards.

Hypothermia or drowning?
Life expectancy in the North Atlantic

In long-term exposure to cold seas it is probable that hypothermia will precede drowning as a cause of death. The importance of heat loss from the body when immersed in cold water was known by the end of the nineteenth century, but hypothermia was not officially considered as a cause of death for the purposes of registering deaths at sea. By far the majority of deaths at sea were attributed to drowning, with thirst and attacks by sharks also given. But when the *Titanic* went down, the conditions were fairly fine and calm with little sea agitation. There were 3,560 lifebelts available for the 1500 or so people who were forced to take to the water. But the fact is by the time the *Carpathia* reached those people (not all of whom wore lifebelts), they were all dead. Yet the official return of deaths by the Superintendent of the Port of Southampton – 19 pages long – lists the cause of death as drowning in every case. Since the ship went down in the vicinity of icebergs it is logical to assess the water was very cold and therefore hypothermia and not drowning was the main cause of death for the vast majority of those lost, floating on the surface of the sea that night.

THE OPPOSITE OF 'OUT OF THE FRYING PAN AND INTO THE FIRE'

Press reports published at the end of April 1912 claimed that a German liner had intercepted wireless traffic between two ships passing not far from the **Titanic***'s last position a fortnight after the sinking, one of which had reported seeing an iceberg with a dozen frozen bodies clustered around its base, wearing lifebelts and huddled close together.*

Water conducts heat away from the human body ten times faster than air. Thus hypothermia can creep up very easily. It is defined as a lowering of the body's core temperature (normally 37 degrees Celsius) caused by heat loss which the body is unable to correct. The body can self-regulate and compensate for slight variations but only to a small extent. It does this by inducing shivering but will then withdraw blood from extremities in order to concentrate warm blood around the vital organs. Hypothermia can be brought on at 36 degrees Celsius. The main areas of the body which lose heat quickly in water are the groin (lots of blood vessels close to the skin); around the chest; and above all, the exposed head and neck (which account for over fifty per cent of the loss). In freezing water, panic and struggling are swiftly followed by a feeling of intense cold and numbness, shortage of breath, weakness and loss of grip, a cessation of shivering as the body conserves what energy is left, followed by incoherence and impaired judgement, confusion and odd behaviour. At a core temperature of 30 degrees or lower it is likely that unconsciousness, heart failure and eventually death will occur. Intake of seawater into the lungs will speed this up and may lead to drowning outright.

Even before death by hypothermia a victim is likely to enter a state where they appear dead but aren't

quite. They are stiff, blue, immobile and their eyes are fixed and pupils dilated. Modern advice is to never assume a person is dead from cold without attempting to re-warm them first. It is probable that some of the *Titanic*'s passengers died after they were picked up, for want of intervention. The sea temperature at the site of the tragedy has been estimated at minus 2 degrees Celsius.

INSULATED BY BOOZE?
Two and a half hours after jumping overboard, Baker Charles Joughin was found treading water nearby collapsible B. Pulled aboard, he ascribed his survival to a bottle of whisky he'd drunk before diving into the sea from the **Titanic.**

*Charles
Joughin*

It is possible that the alcohol in Joughin's bloodstream had lowered his pulse and his metabolic rate, slightly reducing his rate of heat loss and making him a bit calmer than most other people in the water. Given that the expected maximum exposure time before death was estimated at 45 minutes, his survival was heralded as a miracle.

The *Carpathia* to the rescue
Cunard collects the casualties

Carpathia was a Cunard liner carrying 725 passengers en route from New York to the Mediterranean, commanded by the resourceful and respected Captain Arthur Rostron. She was about 50 miles away from *Titanic*'s real as opposed to reported position (which were around 10 miles apart) when she was alerted by *Titanic*'s wireless operators. Ordering wireless operator Cottam to reply with, 'We are coming along as fast as we can' Captain Rostron decided to test his engines like never before and worked his ship up to about 14 knots (not quite the

18 knots claimed afterwards). Even so it would take 3 hours for the ship to reach *Titanic*'s given position, which she did so at approximately 4 a.m., having dodged several icebergs on the way with the help of the six men posted as lookouts.

Carpathia fired rockets every 15 minutes to reassure the *Titanic* she was definitely on her way. At 3.30 a.m. several survivors among the lifeboats thought they saw lightning. This was *Carpathia* still firing rockets as she boiled along at top speed. But crucially Rostron then spotted a green flare set off in Lifeboat 2 a few miles away, and the rescue work began. Had the flare not been set off by Fourth Officer Boxhall on the lifeboat, the *Carpathia* might easily have steamed right past in her haste to find *Titanic*'s wrongly reported

RMS Carpathia

Captain Rostron

The tragic inactivity of the *Californian*
What was she doing?

The Leyland Line's *Californian* was a steamer in the area the night of the sinking. Her actions – or lack of them – have been pored over by maritime historians, scandal-hunters and conspiracy-theorists ever since. Why? Because she was widely accused of having ignored *Titanic's* repeated distress calls, either through misunderstanding or negligence on the part of her crew, commanded by Captain Stanley Lord. Had she been more on the ball, her critics say, she could have helped *Carpathia* rescue many more people once it was clear the *Titanic* was not living up to her billing as one big lifeboat in her own right.

On the Liverpool to Boston run, *Californian* found herself amid an ice field on the evening of 14 April. A cautious skipper, Lord called a halt, signed over control to his Third officer, Charles Groves, and retired to his cabin. At about 11 p.m. Groves spotted the lights of an unidentified ship steaming up from the south east.

position. Overall *Carpathia* managed to rescue 705 passengers and crew. While she was doing so, the *Olympic* arrived on the scene, and offered to take the survivors on to New York. *Carpathia* declined, took one last look around the area for anyone left in the water, exchanged terse messages with the *Californian*, and then at 8.50 a.m. she turned and headed back to port.

DIVINE GUIDE?

'When day broke, I saw the ice I had steamed through during the night. I shuddered, and could only think that some other hand than mine was on that helm during the night.' Captain Arthur Rostron.

Only the *Titanic* was known to be due around these parts. He ordered 20-year-old wireless operator Cyril Evans to contact the *Titanic* to warn her of the ice all around. This was the message which got short shrift from Phillips ('Shut up. Shut up...'), whose ears were blasted by the transmission, thereby leaving unconfirmed as *Titanic* the identity of the ship Groves could see.

Californian was approximately 10 miles away when *Titanic* struck the iceberg at 11.40 p.m. Groves correctly estimated the 'mystery ship' he had seen was a passenger ship about 10 miles away. Captain Lord thought it was a smaller freighter, half that distance away, and went back to his cabin, telling Groves and his relief Second officer Herbert Stone to inform him if the ship moved. At 12.15 a.m., while wireless operator Evans was not at the set, Groves played with it, trying to raise the *Titanic*. While he did this, he missed *Titanic's* first distress signal. Over the next hour and a half, the officers on *Californian's* bridge observed a number of white rockets going up. When they tried to signal to the

vessel firing them using a Morse lamp, they received no reply. The *Californian's* log would never record any sightings of rockets or lights the whole night.

Ship's apprentice Gibson took a look through a pair of binoculars and thought he saw the unknown vessel listing. Other officers assumed that the perspective meant the ship was probably a sailing vessel moving off. Between 2 a.m. and 3 a.m. the duty officers continued to watch the ship in the distance until she disappeared completely from view. This was the *Titanic* sinking beneath the waves.

At 4 a.m. the *Californian's* Chief Officer George Stewart arrived on the bridge. Duty officer Stone reported to him the night's events as they both observed the *Carpathia* moving on the horizon. Checking

SS Californian

with Stone that the vessel they could see was not the same one observed throughout the small hours, Stewart received the reply that no, this was another ship. Stewart felt uneasy at that point, and woke Captain Lord to discuss what they would do next. Lord looked at the *Carpathia* and said 'Well, she looks all right now'. At 5.20 a.m., with a sinking feeling in the pit of his stomach, Stewart woke wireless operator Evans and told him to get on the radio and find out what had been happening. Evans was finally informed by *Frankfort*, *Mount Temple* and *Virginian* that the *Titanic* had sunk during the night, a few miles from their position. By 6 a.m. – over 5 hours after the *Titanic* had issued her first call for help – the *Californian*, under the command of a horrified and guilty-feeling Captain Lord and crew, was on its way to the co-ordinates every rescuer was working from. Yet it took another 2 hours of slow and deliberate navigation through ice to get to the correct spot, where *Carpathia* had been for nearly 4 hours already. *Californian* arrived on the scene just as the *Carpathia* collected the last of the survivors. She

found no additional survivors left to rescue, nor bodies to retrieve.

When the *Californian* arrived in Boston on the morning of 19 April, her crew were questioned about the events of 14 and 15 April. None of the crew admitted to having seen any lights or rockets the entire night. The failure of the *Californian* to react to the disaster unfolding right before them remains among the most tragic aspects of the night.

The news spreads...
Inaccurately

As soon as the first of *Titanic*'s wireless messages was sent out, its signals and those that followed were collected by many radio operators across the eastern seaboard of North America. Associated Press were first off the mark, issuing a note at 1.20 a.m. on 15 April – an hour before she sank – that the *Titanic* had hit an iceberg and was calling for help. Information was fed to the press and, without a single source of authoritative information, confusion reigned. Newspapers, ever on the lookout for a scoop, leapt to conclusions of all kinds based on dubious snippets of information in order to be off the printing presses and onto the streets first. One such example was the headline of the *New York Evening Sun's* final edition of 15 April: 'All Saved from *Titanic* after Collision: Rescue by *Carpathia* and *Parisian*; liner is being towed to Halifax after smashing into an iceberg.'

The *Wall Street Journal* was another to flip a coin and err on the side of hubristic optimism in its editorial piece: 'The gravity of the damage to the *Titanic* is apparent, but the important point is that she did not sink. Her watertight bulkheads were really watertight... Man is the weakest and most formidable creature on the earth. His physical means of protection and offense are trifling. But his brain has within it the spirit of the divine and he overcomes natural obstacles by thought, which is incomparably the greatest force in the universe.'

As the *Carpathia* left the scene of the disaster, Ismay had sent a message to the White Star Line offices: 'Deeply regret advise you *Titanic* sank this

Front page of The New York Herald

morning after collision with iceberg, resulting in serious loss of life. Full particulars later.' When the White Star office in New York found out from *Carpathia* what the real truth was it issued a public rebuke to whoever had spread false rumours already reported as fact: 'Whoever sent this message under the circumstances, is guilty of the most reprehensible conduct.' However, White Star Line could hardly claim to have told the truth right from the off. In a classic example of fruitless damage-limitation, company vice president Philip Franklin put on a brave face as he was besieged while arriving at his New York offices at 8 a.m. on 15 April. Asked if he could comment on the rumours, he announced that the *Titanic* was believed to be unsinkable. That evening, word reached the press from *Olympic* about the real state of affairs. And yet White Star continued to deny the truth until at 7 p.m. Franklin admitted that the ship had sunk. An hour later, he tried to imply that the *Olympic*'s news had not included word that all the crew were saved. Fifteen minutes later, under pressure he admitted that a number of lives had been lost. By 9 p.m. he had changed his tune to 'a horrible loss of life'.

BRITISH NEWSPAPERS FOLLOW SUIT

In the absence of concrete information from White Star or anywhere else in America, British newspapers were not immune from printing the exact opposite of the truth in heartbreaking style, as this front page detail from the **Daily Mirror** *of 16 April shows:*

'Many steamers rushed to her aid, but her fate and that of the thousands on board remained in doubt on both sides of the Atlantic for many hours. It was at length known that every soul was safe, and that the vessel itself was proceeding to Halifax either under her own steam or towed by the Allan liner **Virginian.** *All her passengers had by that time been taken aboard two of the liners that hurried to the scene in reply to the wireless message. They are due at Halifax (Nova Scotia) today and will be taken thence by train to New York. Last night direct news from the* **Titanic** *was received by the parents of the wireless operator on board, who announced cheerfully that the boat was practically unsinkable and that she was making slowly for Halifax.'*

This can only have made the discovery of the awful truth even more horrifying. Only the *New York Times* got it right. The rest scrambled to 'adjust' their stories in the days that followed, in many cases necessitating a complete U-turn on previous reporting and editorial lines.

The *Mackay-Bennett* and Halifax
Bringing the dead back to shore

In the early days after the disaster it was imperative that as many of the bodies could be retrieved as soon as possible. The tragedy had touched thousands of people around the world and they wanted to be able to lay their family or friends to rest or at least achieve some sort of closure. Identification of remains would grow a lot tougher once bodies had been exposed to the potential ravaging effect of weather and predation by birds and sea-life. The bodies would still be relatively clustered together in groups, making the task easier the earlier it was started. Sightings of wreckage and bodies had been made by a variety of ships going about their business, and the area across which this was happening was growing larger. If bodies made their way into the path of the Gulf Stream they might never be found. The *Mackay-Bennett* set out on Wednesday 17 April to commence her sad task, the crew being paid double-time for volunteering. She arrived in the area three days later and began to pick up corpses, numbering 51 of which half were unidentifiable. By a week later, the vessel had 190 bodies aboard and had recommitted another 116 to the sea. Two other vessels found a further 20 bodies between them. Halifax would have a grim task on its hands when the boats came in. The city's ice-rink was told to prepare for the arrival of a lot of bodies: it would double as a makeshift morgue.

NUMBERS ON A GRANITE BLOCK
Halifax, Nova Scotia, became the focal point of efforts to recover the dead of **Titanic** *in the days and weeks after the sinking. As time wore on and hope of finding any survivors dwindled, the gruesome task of trying to identify the corpses took up most of the recovery parties' time. On one such occasion over half of the bodies fished out of the sea by specially chartered vessels like the* **Mackay-Bennett** *were so badly disfigured or decomposed that it proved impossible to find out who they might be. Rather than ferry these poor dead back to shore, the teams simply bagged them*

up in canvas sheets, weighted them with iron bars and sent them back into the ocean for a burial at sea. Of the 150 people recovered to Halifax, nearly half were unidentifiable and they are each commemorated ashore in Fairview Lawn, Baron de Hirsch or Mount Olivet cemeteries, marked by a granite stone bearing the presumed date of their death and their number indicating the order in which they were recovered. One grave in particular aroused much grief – that of an unknown child aged two. No identity could be ascertained until 2002 when DNA revealed that the child belonged to a Swedish woman, Alma Pålsson who was known to have perished with her four young children, and who had been buried near the grave of the unknown child, now identified as Gosta Pålsson. None of the bodies of her other children were ever found.

WHAT HAPPENED TO THE SURVIVORS ONCE THEY REACHED NEW YORK?

It depended on their class and their health. The Carpathia arrived into New York at 9 p.m. on Thursday 18 April. Given that she was carrying more than the passengers she originally intended to land in the US, and could not possibly supply accurate information on all of them, technically she was required to submit to detailed bureaucratic processes in place to deal with aliens. White Star Line wrote to the immigration authorities in Washington to ask for special treatment of the case. This was given assent. As a result, formalities for nearly all First and Second class survivors were carried out aboard the Carpathia. The healthy, wealthy and well-connected were free to leave, and many disappeared as quickly as they could into their own private transport, relieved to see the back of the sea for a while. Since Ellis Island

Ellis Island

was already closed for the night, the ill were transferred to hospitals ashore, but by 25 April most of them had been cleared to leave. All the while, newspaper hacks eager for information descended on as many survivors as they could find, waving $50 bills

and demanding eyewitness accounts. Meanwhile, American authorities immediately began to draw up plans to fathom what went wrong, why and how it could be prevented from ever happening again.

Titanic's grim statistics
Who lived and who died

Titanic passengers: rescued and lost

Category	No. sailed	No. survived	% survived	No. died	% died
First class	329	199	60.5%	130	39.5%
Second class	285	119	41.7%	166	58.3%
Third class	710	174	24.5%	536	75.5%
Crew	899	214	23.8%	685	76.2%
Total	2,223	706	31.8%	1,517	68.2%

Statistics by class:
FIRST CLASS
Sailed:

Men	173
Women and children	156
Total	329

Survived:

Men	54
Women and children	145
Total	199

Surviving officers from Titanic

Died:

Men	119
Women and children	11
Total	130

SECOND CLASS

Sailed:

Men	157
Women and children	128
Total	285

Survived:

Men	15
Women and children	104
Total	119

Died:

Men	142
Women and children	24
Total	166

THIRD CLASS

Sailed:

Men	486
Women and children	224
Total	710

Survived:

Men	69
Women and children	105
Total	174

Died:

Men	417
Women and children	119
Total	536

Popular perception of the disaster is that a higher proportion of Irish steerage passengers died than any other group. In fact the opposite is borne out by the statistics: Irish passengers were less likely to perish than any of their counterparts of other nationalities in steerage. Of approximately 113 Irish passengers in Third class, 40 of them were saved, equating to a survival rate of just over 35 per cent. One hundred non-Irish and non-British steerage passengers were saved out of 410, representing a survival rate of over 24 per cent. In comparison, British passengers in Third class numbered 187, of whom just 38 lived – a survival rate of 20 per cent, the lowest among all Third class passenger groups.

A further surprising statistical reality is that just under 10 per cent of Second class male passengers survived, compared to 14 per cent of all Third class males. The males most likely to survive were of course in First class, with approximately 31 per cent saved. Ninety-three per cent of First class women and children were saved, compared to 81 per cent of Second class and 47 per cent of Third class. It seems that to have been a Second class male aboard the *Titanic* was to run the highest risk of death.

The authorities investigate
The US and British inquiries

The American inquiry began on 19 April and ended on 25 May 1912, a total of 18 days. Led by Senator William Alden Smith, the US inquiry started with J Bruce Ismay

William Alden Smith

and ended up interviewing 86 people in total. Heading for New York on the *Carpathia*, Ismay had hoped to escape the attention of the US authorities, and, using a ridiculous attempt at a pseudonym – 'Yamsi' – signalled to the effect that he wanted all British survivors put on the first boat back to Britain. Intercepting these signals, Smith and his committee high-tailed it to New York and stepped on board the *Carpathia* as soon as she docked, subpoenas in hand. The resulting inquiry transcript runs to over a thousand pages. Ismay's testimony makes up 58 of them.

THE WORLD'S MOST LUXURIOUS DISASTER INQUIRY
In 1897, John Jacob Astor IV built the Astoria Hotel on Park Avenue in New York, reputedly the world's most luxurious hotel at the time. This adjoined the Waldorf Hotel, already built by Astor's cousin, William Waldorf Astor; later the combined premises became known as the Waldorf-Astoria Hotel, which boasted a thousand bedrooms and still touts itself as a beacon of old-world

*elegance in the bustling metropolis. Ironically the hotel became the location of the American authorities' inquiries into the sinking of the **Titanic**.*

The Waldorf-Astoria

Stung into action by the irritating zeal with which the American Senate was probing the disaster – a predominantly British matter, so they thought – the British inquiry started on 2 May and ended on 3 July 1912, a total of 36 days. Ordered by the Board of Trade, in charge was Charles Bigham, Lord Mersey of Toxteth, President of the Probate, Divorce and Admiralty Division of the High Court, assisted by five maritime and

naval experts. It was held at the drill hall of the London Scottish Regiment in Buckingham Gate, Westminster. Over the course of the inquiry, 96 witnesses including Ismay would be asked 25,622 questions.

X MARKS THE SPOT

*The 1912 British Board of Trade's inquiry called 96 surviving witnesses to give testimony about their experiences during the tragedy, in an attempt to uncover as much information as possible about the cause of the accident, the reaction of the officers and crew, the conduct of the passengers and so on. To assist the witnesses, some of whom were reportedly illiterate, a 10-metre 3/8 inch-to-1-foot scale cross-section profile drawing in Indian ink of the **Titanic** was created by the White Star Line architects' department and hung in the inquiry room at the London Scottish drill hall for the 36-day duration. Using a pointer and the diagram, evidence could be illustrated, locations ascertained and sequences of events clarified. Once the inquiry had concluded, the unique plan was returned to White Star. It* *remained in private ownership since then; in May 2011 it changed hands at auction in the UK for £220,000. Red and green chalk marks remain on the drawing indicating where the Titanic's hull was thought to have struck the iceberg.*

The American inquiry ended on 25 May. Its findings were that the *Titanic* was going too fast with an inadequate lookout; lifeboat loading and lowering was shambolic; the *Californian* was guilty of seeing the distress rockets and failing to act; and that there was no deliberate discrimination against Third class passengers. The US inquiry interviewed only three Third class passengers, three more than the British inquiry called; that said, all three testified that they had not been discriminated against.

BEESLEY'S JUSTIFICATION

In the preface to his bestselling account of the disaster compiled and published in mid-1912, 34-year-old Second class survivor and Cambridge scholar Lawrence Beesley opined: 'Whoever reads the account of the

cries that came to us afloat on the sea from those sinking in the ice-cold water must remember that they were addressed to him just as much as to those who heard them, and that the duty of seeing that reforms are carried out devolves on every one who knows that such cries were heard in utter helplessness the night the **Titanic sank.'**

At the end of the British deliberations on 3 July, which seemed to many a whitewash for failing to directly finger Ismay and White Star for their failings (sanctioned implicitly by the regulatory environment laid down by the British Board of Trade), the US findings were agreed and a number of further recommendations were made. First, passenger ships should carry enough lifeboats for all aboard. Secondly, there should be more thorough and more frequent lifeboat drills. Thirdly, the quality of watertight bulkheads should be improved. And fourthly, all wireless sets should be manned 24 hours a day. In fact, Phillips and Bride were already operating under that arrangement, agreed between them.

But, crucially, the *Californian*, with its sole wireless operator, had not been able to do the same. Ninety minutes after Evans had powered down his set and gone to bed the first of *Titanic*'s distress calls was broadcast from only a few miles away.

Later, the 'Southern track' Edward Smith had followed was moved about 230 miles further south and east to better avoid the risk of ice, and an international ice patrol was established at the International Convention for the Safety of Life at Sea in early 1914; the patrol has operated ever since, and annually lays a wreath in commemoration of the *Titanic* at the spot of her sinking.

Taking the rough with the smooth
How did White Star treat Third class passengers?

The clearest sign we have that Third class passengers were not deliberately prevented from getting to the boats is that those women and children from steerage who made it up from below were allowed to board lifeboats ahead of men of all classes.

But why did segregation of the travelling classes even exist?

American immigration laws were strict and passenger lines taking the emigrant trade were expected to abide by them, on pain of expensive fines and loss of service. The laws were designed to maintain reasonable standards of conditions for steerage passengers, and they included restrictions on the accommodation and movement of steerage passengers aboard ship. The prevention of the spreading of disease – from passenger to passenger, class to class, ship to shore – was another, less overtly stated aim. Thus any emigrant ship landing in the USA found to be without barriers (or not using them in line with the law) was liable to be forced into quarantine for over a month. This did not look good for the company and cost a lot of money. As a matter of abiding with the law, most passenger ship firms made sure that their vessels complied as far as they could with the US authorities' strictures. This could be done by altering the internal structure of the ship to make Third class physically distant from the rest of the passenger accommodation by inserting well decks between the upper decks and the main deck on which the steerage passengers were accommodated, but this was not always feasible or desirable. Instead, or in addition, many lines opted for a system of gates.

Testimony from survivors in Third class occasionally refers to small lockable metal gates that led from lower decks to higher decks, informal waist-high barriers and emergency doors. The mere presence of gates to keep people apart on the same ship strikes many people today as an act of discrimination. But in general Third class passengers were well-catered for on White Star vessels. Testimony from them indicates that their berths were well-ventilated, sanitary yet offered reasonable privacy; food was simple but wholesome and plentiful; spacious and well-fitted public common rooms were provided; and the class had its own open deck areas to roam across without interference from the crew. In fact, in relative terms the steerage passengers' experience aboard *Titanic* was probably superior to that enjoyed by the other classes. It would therefore be a stretch to say that the

White Star line short-changed its steerage passengers or discriminated against them in general. It would not have struck the steerage passengers as odd or unusual that they were not expected to mingle with the cabin classes. It is worth pointing out that Second class passengers were also restricted in their movements around the ship; First class areas were out of bounds – and of course the same concept operates today aboard train carriages, airliners and VIP lounges.

But what about when emigration turned into evacuation? At 12.30 a.m. the order was given – though doubtlessly not received by all – to start passing up women and children from Third class. This 50-minute period between the collision and the order is evidence to some that Third class lives were not a priority. But the fact is that this was still ten minutes before the first lifeboat was lowered. In any case, it is true that some but not all stewards unlocked gates and opened up passageways so Second and Third class passengers could move up to the boat deck. However, there are accounts of individuals or groups of passengers being temporarily held below decks while others were allowed to make their way up the boat deck. Walter Lord famously recounts the anecdote of Irishman Jim Farrell, who coming across three female compatriots being held behind a gate, roared at the man guarding it: 'Great God, man! Open the gate and let the girls through!' The sailor manning it complied immediately. In addition, several accounts – from both steerage and First class eyewitnesses – describe a 'mass of people' rushing up from below decks at the last minute, far too late to get off via lifeboat. Is this attributable to locked gates? If so, why did some barriers still remain locked after the collision?

It cannot be because the ship's officers wished to put the requirements of US immigration law above everything else. It is also unlikely that *Titanic*'s chain of command wished to prevent steerage passengers from reaching the boats. Rather, it is likely that much of the attention of the officers and crew was focused individually on the need to react to the collision, and in the chaos and confusion the male steerage passengers were, for reasons

of women and children first, not the primary consideration. Some gates were missed and as a result of this, and the generally disorganised state of affairs, men in steerage were forced to fend for themselves. The sudden surge of people is most likely due to the ship beginning to break up, causing those who had sought shelter below to fight for their escape.

Hindsight is a wonderful thing
The question of Captain Smith's negligence

S urely Captain Smith ought to have slowed *Titanic* down in the knowledge that ice might lie ahead? Well, unless a ship's lookouts could actually see substantial ice in the way – big enough to risk damage to the vessel – it was not normal practice for liners to slow down in clear weather just because of reports of ice. Several masters of enormous collective experience on the North Atlantic shipping routes testified at the inquiries and all agreed that prior to the *Titanic* disaster no captain would give the order to slow down in clear conditions after an ice warning unless ice could be seen in the ship's path. Given that Smith perceived the ship's route to be southerly enough to avoid any large ice fields, and that conditions were deemed clear, his decision to maintain speed on a commercially important maiden voyage is understandable. That it was the *Titanic* that collided with an iceberg at high speed and was lost was Smith and his passengers' terrible luck, and shows that the common practice was not safe after all.

As Lord Mersey, the British Wreck Commissioner, put it in his final report: '... the practice of liners using this track when in the vicinity of ice at night had been in clear weather to keep the course, to maintain the speed and to trust to a sharp look-out to enable them to avoid the danger. This practice, it was said, had been justified by experience, no casualties having resulted from it... But the event has proved the practice to be bad. Its root is probably to be found in competition and in the desire of the public for quick passages rather than in the judgement of navigators. But unfortunately experience

appeared to justify it. In these circumstances I am not able to blame Captain Smith... he was doing only that which other skilled men would have done in the same position... He made a mistake, a very grievous mistake, but one in which, in face of the practice and of past experience, negligence cannot be said to have had any part; and in the absence of negligence it is, in my opinion, impossible to fix Captain Smith with blame... What was a mistake in the case of the *Titanic* would without doubt be negligence in any similar case in the future.'

Smith's widow Eleanor took a broader view and offered the following sentiment: 'To my poor fellow-sufferers: my heart overflows with grief for you all and is laden with sorrow that you are weighed down with this terrible burden that has been thrust upon us. May God be with us and comfort us all.'

THE QUALITY OF MERSEY

*In early May, London's satirical magazine **Punch** commented on the Wreck Commissioner's proceedings:*

'*Americans would do well to note that the British way, when a Commission of Enquiry is appointed, is to temper justice with Mersey.*'

Renault town car

Anyone seen my Marmalade Machine?
The curious possessions lost aboard Titanic

Leaving aside the obvious human tragedy inherent in the lives lost in the *Titanic* disaster, there were substantial material losses too. *Titanic* was not insured against the loss of her cargo (and was covered for only two-thirds of her £1,500,000 building cost). A list of the most interesting cargo claimed to have been lost with the ship – produced for the benefit of the insurers – includes some bizarre, esoteric and exotic items, as well as the more mundane. Over 3,000 bags of mail and an estimated 800 parcels were lost, despite the gallant efforts of the mailmen aboard (they all perished). Several tons of unconsumed food and drink went to the bottom. A 35 horsepower 1912 Renault Towncar purchased in France

and belonging to wealthy passenger William Carter went down, while its owner survived. Sadly there is no evidence to say that this was the car romped in by Jack Dawson and Rose DeWitt Bukater in Cameron's *Titanic* (1997). Five grand pianos and four cases of opium disappeared. Thirty cases of golf clubs and tennis racquets earmarked for Boston Red Stockings pitcher and sports equipment retailer Albert Goodwill Spalding sank to the seabed, along with 96 tennis balls. Several crates of ancient artefacts destined for the Colorado Museum of Natural History in Denver went down. A bejewelled copy of the *Rubaiyyat of Omar Khayyam* was lost. Newspapers at the time reported that 'there was known to be a small fortune in diamonds aboard the *Titanic*'; there were also reports of wealthy individuals choosing to travel in lower classes to avoid notice while carrying expensive valuables. Many examples of diamonds, jewels and keepsakes were recovered from bodies picked up by the *Mackay-Bennett*, the Halifax-based cable-ship turned chartered recovery vessel. A crewman told the press that while inspecting the pockets of one man, 'seventeen diamonds rolled out in every direction upon the littered deck.' Other fine jewellery recovered from expeditions to the wreck includes a bracelet with the name 'Amy' inscribed in gemstones. Despite rumours stoked by the 1997 film *Titanic*, no Picassos or Monets were harmed in the making of the movie, nor in real life. But a Mrs Edwina Trout lost her beloved Marmalade Machine.

The tangled bureaucracy of death
Why the official tolls don't match up

You'd be forgiven for assuming that in the cold light of day a century on it's a relatively simple matter to find out who lived and who died on the *Titanic*. To establish the names of the victims, surely you take the ship's register of embarked passengers and crew and, through a straightforward process of deduction, remove the names of the survivors picked up by the *Carpathia*, right? Well, in theory. But not one but upwards of a dozen different official lists existed in relation to various aspects of *Titanic*'s passengers. Many may still be consulted in archives today. Each was compiled as an official record for a specific purpose. That said, might it not be reasonable to expect that these various lists would be identical, given that they originated in the offices of the shipping company or government authorities accustomed to keeping accurate records of maritime movements? A list is a list, after all. But none of these lists can be thought of as complete, definitive and accurate across the board. Why not?

The fact is that various different bodies and authorities not only in Britain but in the US and Canada required lists to be compiled in advance of any ocean-bound voyage.

In *Titanic*'s case – though by no means out of the ordinary – this included tallies of tickets sold before the voyage; of the crew and passengers going aboard the *Titanic* at Southampton; of passengers joining at Cherbourg and Queenstown; of the immigrants expected by authorities in New York; of those passengers intending to travel on to other final destinations. Due to the calamitous turn of events, other much less routine lists suddenly became necessary and urgent – of passengers who unexpectedly arrived in the USA on the *Carpathia* instead of the *Titanic*; of passenger casualties and deaths at sea; of bodies actually recovered, identified, and dispositions of; employees' loss in service; valuations for insurance purposes, and so on.

The Marine Department of the British Board of Trade; the office of the Superintendent of the Marine Office in Southampton; White Star Line's office in Southampton; the British Registrar General of Shipping and Seamen; the purser of the *Carpathia*; Ellis Island immigration authorities in New York; Canadian delegated immigrant authorities from Halifax in New York – all were

required to produce accurate lists of passengers and crew according to their particular area of authority, whether as routine pre-voyage administration or as shocked post-disaster reckoning.

Consequently, records meeting different purposes proliferated. While some were already stored by the time the vessel set sail, those compiled after the disaster did not always benefit from the luxury of time and space to chase down all the information. Human error crept in. Details given by survivors under shock and stress aboard the *Carpathia* were, understandably, not wholly reliable or consistent. And investigating authorities in the US and Britain were not always able to cross-reference one list against another, in some cases entirely failing to consult earlier accounts. On the other hand, the White Star Line, the Board of Trade and the Registrar General of Shipping and Seamen inevitably conferred on their data, leading to a mass of pooled correspondence and risking cross-contamination of record-keeping. Great pressure was placed on the authorities on both sides of the Atlantic to come up with a reconciled tally that showed exactly who had died and who had survived. The calculations were by no means straightforward. The overall result is that any two or more entries for the same individual person are seldom found to be identical across the available different lists.

PASSENGER NAMES ADD TO THE CONFUSION

The presence of so many foreign names among the passengers (mostly travelling in Third class) gave the investigators a real problem when it came to reconciling passenger lists. Accustomed to the English-language naming convention – surname and given name – the intricacies of global naming practices, with variations in languages, spellings, pronunciations, even indecipherable hand-writing, would likely have been a headache for the shipping clerks whose job it was to enter details of embarking passengers onto lists. Much like the situation found in parish records in Britain which can show surnames evolving over quite short periods of time, the clerks generally tried their best to capture the correct details and must be given leeway in having to rely on their own interpretations at times. With this in mind it is clear that investigating officials trying to tidy up and finalise the records after the fact faced quite a challenge in arriving at definitive accuracy.

To take the example of casualty lists, the speedy production of an accurate record of souls lost aboard the *Titanic* was rightly deemed desirable by the Registrar General of Shipping and Seamen in London, whose responsibility it was to provide the final reckoning in order to: officially register the many deaths among passengers and crew; provide evidence for the Board of Trade Inquiry; and register an entry in the Board of Trade's Wreck Register. So, a list isn't just a list after all.

Southampton mourns
A fitting maritime memorial

A large proportion of *Titanic's* crew were Southampton-based and the shock of the loss of 549 of them was keenly felt by the city on many levels, not least by the wives and families of men who were never to return to their tightly-knit communities. To commemorate the heroism of the crew, in particular the engineers who to a man were lost while battling so hard to keep the *Titanic* afloat and with power so her passengers could get off, a grand monument was raised in Southampton's East Park, just as other monuments sprang up all over Britain. In April 1914, almost two years to the day after the disaster, a grand memorial was unveiled by Sir Archibald Denny, President of the Institute of Marine Engineers. As the Union flag draped over the edifice was removed, Denny revealed the bold design to the huge crowd of 100,000 or so Southampton citizen onlookers and offered the following words:

'By the manner of their deaths [the engineers] carried out one of the finest traditions of our race. They must have known that pumping could do no more than delay the final catastrophe, yet they stuck pluckily to their duty. Driven back from boiler-room to boiler-room, fighting for every inch of draught to give time for the launching of the boats, not one of those brave officers was saved.'

The monument is there to this day. Depicting the winged goddess Nike riding on the prow of a ship, the granite and bronze work bears the names of the engineers and the following inscription:

'Greater love hath no man than this, that a man lay down his life for his friends.'

'To the memory of the engineer officers of the RMS *Titanic,* who showed their high conception of duty and their heroism by remaining at their posts 15th April 1912.'

'Erected by their fellow engineers and friends on 22nd April 1914.'

Connections with Southampton permeated the ship and the city is home to a number of further memorials, including one for the *Titanic*'s musicians. Originally erected in Southampton's Old Library, it was destroyed by bombing in the Second World War but a replica was re-dedicated in 1990 in the company of four surviving passengers. Among its features is an inscription of the opening bars of the hymn 'Nearer My

God to Thee'. The High Street Post Office carried a plaque in honour and remembrance of the five men who manned the *Titanic*'s on-board postal office. The plaque is fashioned from metal from a spare propeller donated by Harland and Wolff.

IN MEMORIAM

The number of memorials is thought to now surpass 700 following the centenary of the sinking as communities re-remembered those involved. Most of them are in Britain and Ireland. This number is expected to surpass 700 as the centenary of the sinking is reached and communities re-remember those involved.

William T Stead has a bronze memorial plaque on the Victoria embankment in London not far from Fleet Street, the traditional home of London's newspaper industry for many years. The memorial celebrates his tireless work in what might today be dubbed 'investigative journalism' – which frequently saw him clash with the authorities in pursuit of peace, greater social justice for children, the poor, and greater rights for women. But oddly there is no mention of his

death on the **Titanic,** *beyond the year '1912'. A similar memorial at New York's Fifth Avenue and 91st Street does refer to his death. An interesting link exists between the loss to British life and prestige occasioned by the* **Titanic** *disaster and the death of polar explorer Captain Robert Falcon Scott, RN, who perished a month earlier in March 1912 in heroic circumstances having failed to be first to reach the South Pole. Both losses made headlines in Britain and around the world, and seemed in hindsight to signal the close of a long and stable*

A memorial to William T. Stead

chapter in British history, before the outbreak of the First World War in August 1914 set the seal on it. In July 1914 a large statue of Captain Edward Smith was unveiled in Lichfield. The sculptor was Lady Kathleen Scott, widow of Scott of the Antarctic.

Robert Falcon Scott

Cold steel
Was the Titanic*'s hull too brittle in cold water?*

According to research published in 1998 in the Journal of Metallurgy, the steel used by Harland and Wolff in the construction of Titanic's hull had what is called a 'high

ductile-brittle transition temperature', which meant it was less able to deform without breaking and made it unsuitable (to modern standards) for use at low temperatures. Given that the temperature of the water at the site of the iceberg collision was minus 2 Celsius, questions have been raised as to whether the great ship was unnecessarily vulnerable to the effects of a collision with anything in very cold water. But importantly the research concluded that the builders had little or no choice. Like most steel at the time, it was produced in open-hearth furnaces which permitted the entry of impurities like phosphorous and sulphur into the composition. And like all shipbuilders, Titanic's builders wished to use the best materials available. In 1909-11, the steel they used, supplied by Dalzell and Colvilles, was probably the best plain carbon ship plate available. However, today it would not be recommended for any structural purposes including shipbuilding.

As the ship flooded, an estimated maximum 'bending moment' of over 5 million foot-tons was created. The strength of Titanic's steel was no match for it. In fact, no ship could withstand that amount of stress and survive.

Had the *Titanic* enjoyed modern navigational aids it is likely that the ship would have pursued a long career, just like the *Olympic* – built by the same yard from the same materials – was able to. The *Queen Mary*, which survives even now, was built for the amalgamated Cunard White Star Line from steel produced by the same mill as that which was used to construct *Titanic*.

RMS Olympic's *'new' lifeboats*

OLYMPIC AFTER THE *TITANIC*

After the tragic demise of her sister-ship, **Olympic** *was brought into dry dock and underwent a number of safety improvements, chiefly the retrofitting of an inner watertight skin, new watertight bulkheads extending higher in the ship, and provision of 43 lifeboats, enough for all passengers. With these changes she increased her weight to 46,359 tons, 31 more than* **Titanic**.

After an unhappy 'mutiny' by 276 of Olympic's crew at the condition of the 'new' lifeboats put aboard (they were in a pretty poor state, recycled from older liners), she continued her transatlantic passenger service under Captain James Haddock until three years later, when in September 1915 she was requisitioned by the British Admiralty for service as a troopship and received a coat of dazzle camouflage paint intended to confuse enemy submarines, one of which (U-103) she successfully spotted, turned towards, rammed and sank in May 1918, becoming the only merchantman to sink an enemy vessel in the whole war. This episode neatly demonstrates that the **Olympic** *class – all equipped with the same size and shape of rudder – enjoyed responsive controls and effective manoeuvrability. It has been calculated that under Admiralty orders* **Olympic** *carried* *up to 201,000 troops and other personnel, burning 347,000 tons of coal and steaming about 184,000 nautical miles in the process. After the war she returned to regular passenger service and worked until her final voyage to Southampton in 1935, garnering the nickname of 'Old Reliable'. However, she didn't entirely escape further tragedy. In May 1934, as she approached New York in thick fog, Olympic collided with the Nantucket lightship, effectively cutting it in half. Of the lightship's crew of ten, four drowned, three were fatally wounded, and three were saved.*

It's all a question of luck
The indomitable Violet Jessop

Violet Constance Jessop was a determined and plucky lady. Depending on your viewpoint she was also either the luckiest or the unluckiest employee of White Star ever to sail their fleet of giants. She was born in 1887 in Argentina to Irish parents but later moved to Britain. As a child she survived

tuberculosis. In October 1910 she boarded the *Olympic* as a stewardess. Eleven months later the *Olympic*, outbound from Southampton to New York, collided with HMS *Hawke* in the Solent, sustaining serious damage. Then, on 10 April 1912, Miss Jessop stepped aboard the *Titanic* at Southampton, again as a stewardess.

FEMALE CREW
Titanic's crew numbered 899. Of these, only 23 were women. All were stewardess like Violet Jessop except for two restaurant cashiers, a Turkish bath attendant, a matron in Third class and a masseuse. Given the 'women and children' first policy in force aboard ship in time of calamity, it would be reasonable to expect that all of the female crew would have got off the ship. After all, over 23 per cent of the crew managed to escape with their lives. Unfortunately, three of the women crew died: stewardesses Lucy Snape and Katherine Walsh, and Third class matron Catherine Wallis.

Four and a half days later she found herself rushing up onto the boat deck in the night air, ordered to do so by her manager so she could set a good example to the foreign steerage passengers as the crew set about loading lifeboats. She clambered into Lifeboat 16 and was handed a baby to look after. Her lifeboat was picked up by the *Carpathia* the next day. Violet reported that while on board her rescue ship bound for New York, an unidentified woman snatched the baby she was holding and ran off without word of explanation. She never saw either of them again, but many years later she was intrigued to receive a late night telephone call from a woman claiming to be the baby Violet had rescued. Her biographer brushed it off as a hoax, but Violet maintained that she had never told anyone about it before.

And to top it all off, she was employed as a Red Cross nurse aboard the converted hospital ship and third *Olympic* class ship *Britannic* when it sank after being struck by a mine or torpedo in the Aegean in late 1916, becoming the biggest ship to be lost during the war. According to her testimony she leapt out of a lifeboat to avoid being pulled into one of *Britannic's* still-revolving propellers.

Violet Jessop

In doing so, she was sucked down under water and hit her head on the ship's keel before being plucked out of the sea. She attributed her survival to her thick head of auburn hair. In fact, she had fractured her skull and only found out years later. Incredibly, she continued to work for passenger lines – including White Star, until 1935, clocking up an incredible 55 completed (and two aborted) voyages in their service. She finally retired from the sea in 1950.

THE GIGANTIC BRITANNIC
The myth goes that, launched on 26 February 1914, Titanic's second

sister-ship was supposed originally to be named **Gigantic** but, possibly chastened by the loss of her elder sister (and with the knowledge that other nations were building yet-bigger ships), White Star decided to play things down by opting for a twice-tried and tested 'lucky' White Star name, **Britannic**. In fact, the weight of the evidence suggests that the name **Britannic** had been earmarked as early as June 1911 when Hull Number 433 was still on the building slip. The largest of the three at 48,158 gross tonnes, externally she was more similar to **Titanic** than **Olympic** – she retained the enclosed A-deck promenade – but visibly carried more lifeboats on more davits. She was equipped with turbines 10 per cent more powerful than **Titanic's** to make up for a hull increase of 2 feet in width, and of course, a double bottom and inner skin were fitted as standard. Watertight bulkheads right up to B deck were also fitted. Sadly they did not prevent **Britannic** from sinking 55 minutes after the explosion in the Aegean. However, in contrast with the **Titanic**, 1,036 men were saved and only thirty lost.

If the ship had been crammed full of patients the story would have been very different. **Olympic** alone remained as the sole survivor of White Star's trio of world-beaters.

On the silver screen
Titanic *in the cinema*

The story of the *Titanic* has it all – death, irony, tragedy, folly, greed, heroism, courage, love, sacrifice, salvation...There is so much, in fact, that the epic truth is usually more dramatic than any fictional reimagining. Among the events of 1912 there is a huge amount of 'human interest' material for practitioners of the arts to draw on, and the ship, her crew and passengers have been the subject of artistic

Dorothy Gibson, Titanic *survivor*

interpretation and memorialisation ever since. It is probably in film that the most memorable dramatic reimagining has been recorded.

That said, the popularity of the story has not been constant over the past hundred years. Aside from a raft of factual presentations featuring cobbled-together newsreel footage of *Olympic* and almost any other large liner, shown in theatres in the weeks after the sinking, an initial flurry of bigger, more exciting films with an element of fiction came out within a year or two of the sinking – 1912's *In Nacht und Eis* (directed by Mime Misu); 10-minute silent film *Saved from the Titanic* (Etienne Arnaud), which featured survivor Dorothy Gibson, wearing the same clothes she had worn on the night of the disaster, and which was reputed to have been shot in a week and released within a month; and 1913's *Atlantis* (August Blom). Blom's film was the first to use two lovers as a mechanism for framing the story, a method which would become familiar down the years.

The disaster was somewhat eclipsed in scale over the next few years by

the outbreak of the First World War in Europe and the Second World War twenty years later. The first sound movie to be made about the ship was 1929's *Atlantic* (Ewald Andre Dupont). A German propaganda film of 1943 (directed by Selpin and Klingler) was the first to use just the ship's name as its title, and also the first – and last – to introduce a completely made-up German officer as a key figure in the ship's crew.

It wasn't until the post-war era that film interpretations of the story became truly popular with two big landmark films: 1953's American melodrama *Titanic* (Jean Negulesco) starring Barbara Stanwyck, Clifton Webb and Robert Wagner, which focused on another couple's story aboard ship; and 1958's more fact-based British production based on Walter Lord's groundbreaking 1955 bestseller, *A Night to Remember*, starring war film legend Kenneth More as Charles Lightoller.

The movie was deliberately shot in black and white to give it a gritty tone. Survivors were interviewed and *Titanic*'s Fourth Officer Joseph Boxhall was used as a technical advisor by the production. The production was one of the first to make use of sets that could be tilted by hydraulic jacks, which not only looked good but made the right sort of loud, creaking noises of a sinking ship. The film won a Golden Globe and has been praised ever since as a high-point of accuracy and realism in the way the *Titanic* story has been presented in the cinema.

DEJA VIEW
Actor Bernard Fox, who appeared uncredited in **A Night to Remember** *as Lookout Fleet, also appeared as Colonel Archibald Gracie in James Cameron's* **Titanic** *of 1997.*

The 1960s, '70s and '80s saw a decline in the interest paid to the topic by Hollywood and other studios. The films made in this period included *The Unsinkable Molly Brown* (1964, Charles Walters) which attempted to replicate the musical theatre of the 1960 play of the same name; and 1980's poorly-received *Raise the Titanic!*

'THEY'VE FOUND THE *TITANIC*. THERE'S ONLY ONE THING LEFT TO DO...'
Of all the numerous attempts to depict the **Titanic** *on the big screen, Jerry Jameson's 1980 offering* **Raise the Titanic!** *– based on the novel by action thriller writer Clive Cussler – was perhaps the most bloated and unsuccessful. The ambitious plot revolved around the efforts of the US Navy to raise the ship in order to retrieve from its cargo hold a rare mineral vital for a new nuclear defence project. To add a dash of Cold War piquancy, the Soviets are also planning to grab the stuff for their own ends. The all-star production's acting, dialogue, plot and special effects – which together cost around $40 million – were almost universally panned, and the film plummeted to an early bath at the box office, recouping less than ten per cent of its costs, and leading to British media mogul and film producer Lew Grade's classic utterance: "Raise the* **Titanic?** *My God, it would be cheaper to lower the Atlantic!"*

The discovery of the *Titanic*'s physical location in the mid-1980s spurred a new round of interest in the vessel and her story. James Cameron became interested in the footage being brought back from the seabed by Robert Ballard and others, and started planning what would become 1997's cinema behemoth starring Kate Winslet and Leonardo DiCaprio. Utilising incredible new special effects and picking the brains of a pre-eminent cast of hired experts, James Cameron created what is undoubtedly the benchmark for blockbusting epic love stories, disaster movies and spin-off industries all rolled into one. In a search for historical accuracy Cameron's production crew made use of blueprints from Harland and Wolff, and Thomas Andrews' own notebook of design features. Cameron hired a Russian submersible to take shots of the ship's fixtures and fittings; as much evidence as possible was gathered on what the interior of the ship looked like, and where possible it was replicated for the sets. Even the original carpet manufacturer – BMK Stoddard – had its 1912 designs on file and reproduced the flooring used onboard.

The production's set at Baja, Mexico, comprised the world's largest seawater shooting tank (holding 64 million litres of water) and a number of other interior and exterior tanks where filming of the giant *Titanic* ship set could be done. The ship set itself was a 236-metre-long exterior model, 30 metres high to the top of the funnels. Interior and exterior sets were built on hydraulic jacks to enable the required influx of water at the correct angles, and hinges in the sets allowed for the breaking up of the ship. But for the really spectacular exterior shots, Cameron turned to CGI. The sheer scope of the production – dictated in no small part by the massive set – allowed for some incredible shots impossible to create in real life yet rendered so accurately as to be indistinguishable from standard film footage. Principal among the shots unique at that time to *Titanic* were the top-down 'fly-around' vistas of the vessel in mid-ocean. Putting down a marker for the grand scale of the real-life disaster and its film representation, these scenes were exhilarating for the audience.

Against early expectations, the film – produced by the Fox and Paramount studios – went on to become the highest-grossing film to date, earning more than $1.843 billion in worldwide box-office receipts, a billion of those by March 1998. The film was reputed to need $400 million of income just to break even! Its position at top spot of the earnings league was not surpassed until 2010 by Cameron's next visually stunning directorial offering, *Avatar*.

Titanic remains the only film of the twentieth century to sit in the list of the top ten grossing films of all time. It garnered eleven Oscars at the 1998 Academy Awards. The tie-in album – featuring the inescapable Celine Dion hit *My Heart Will Go On* – became the biggest-selling movie soundtrack of all time. And to round it all out, the book about the making of the film sat at the top of the *New York Times* bestseller chart for several weeks, the first time such a tie-in publication had reached such a pinnacle. Made-for-TV dramas and special IMAX presentations notwithstanding, no-one has yet dared to launch a big-screen feature film to rival Cameron's category-killer.

Titanic back under the hammer
The trade in memorabilia

The market in '*Titanicania*' began almost as soon as the news of the tragedy hit the shore. It thrives to this day, stoked up by repeated visits by commercial enterprises to the wreck site in search of evocative artefacts and personal curios which can sell for thousands of pounds. There is a large core of dedicated *Titanic* collectors, some of whom are evidently very wealthy individuals or societies. A short list of record-breaking sales at auction would include £51,000 paid in 2004 for a menu for the first dinner ever served aboard *Titanic* on 2 April as she steamed from Belfast to Southampton. It had been sent by Fifth Officer Harold Lowe to his future wife while the ship was off Queenstown. The previous record for a ship's menu was £29,500. In 2010 Devizes-based sale house Henry Aldridge & Son's auctions of *Titanic* and White Star memorabilia broke several other world record prices. These included £62,000 for an authentic promotional poster; £56,000 for a letter penned aboard the ship, £55,000 for a set of keys and £35,000 for a photo of passenger Rhoda Mary 'Rosa' Abbott.

'ROSA' ABBOTT

Rhoda Mary Abbott was an Aylesbury-born woman who had moved to Rhode Island in 1894 where she married a British-born US middleweight boxing champion. Later after the breakdown of her marriage she decided to return to England to live with her mother in St Albans. She and her two teenage sons took passage in 1911 with the **Olympic** *but some time later decided to return to the States. Paying £20 5s for a Third-class ticket aboard the* **Titanic** *– on which her name was recorded in error as 'Rosa' – the three were lucky to make their way as a group up from the steerage accommodation via the Second class saloon and through the controlled gates leading up to the boat deck. Reluctant to leave her sons behind when offered a place in collapsible lifeboat C, she hung back and eventually the three were forced to jump from the deck into a maelstrom of water and bodies as the* **Titanic** *went down beneath them. Unfortunately her two boys were lost but she was pulled into the already-swamped collapsible lifeboat A. She clung on, knee-deep in sea water, through the cold and grief. One of her fellow survivors, August Wennerstrom, recalled the horrific conditions: 'All the feeling left us. If we wanted to know if we still had* *legs left, we had to feel down into the water with our hand. The only exercise we got was when someone gave up hope and died, whom we immediately threw overboard to give the live ones a little more space and at the same time lighten the weight of the boat.' Eventually Rosa transferred into Fifth Officer Lowe's boat and from there into the* **Carpathia.** *Three people – First class passenger Thomson Beattie, and two crew – died during the night aboard collapsible A. Their bodies, still inside the boat, were found by the liner* **Oceanic** *during a transatlantic crossing about a month later. Their remains were buried at sea.*

Secret assignment for Ballard
Cold War casualties are proving ground for Titanic *search*

It is a little-known fact that in 1982 Robert Ballard had asked for funding from the US Navy to help his search for the *Titanic*. This was granted but only on the secret condition that the first priority was to use the resources and technology

to examine the wreckage of the US nuclear submarines USS *Thresher* and USS *Scorpion* which had disappeared at the height of the Cold War, with the loss of more than 200 officers and crew.

Ballard had developed a robotic submarine craft in the early 1980s and approached the US Navy for assistance. According to reports he was told that the military were not willing to spend a fortune on locating the liner, but they did want to know what had happened to their submarines, which still contained their nuclear reactor powerplants. Ballard used his advanced equipment to locate the submerged wrecks, both of which were lying in hundreds of pieces on the sea floor – the *Thresher* in waters

USS *Scorpion*

off the east coast of the USA and the *Scorpion* in the eastern Atlantic.

The *Thresher* had sunk in April 1963 with all hands while undergoing sea trials after dockyard repairs. The likely culprit was a blown pressure pipe supplying the reactor with cooling water, which caused the submarine to lose power and sink so deep that her hull imploded under the pressure. The *Scorpion* disappeared in 1968, leading to speculation that it had fallen victim to action by the Soviet Navy. Ballard's data suggested

Robert Ballard

that the submarine could have been struck by a torpedo fired from its own tubes. The details of the searches, along with the results, remain classified. But the long trails of debris which Ballard saw around the two submarine wrecks encouraged him to look for similar around the *Titanic*'s last known position.

Scattered across the sea-bed
The resting places of the wreck

At 1.05 in the morning of 1 September 1985 the remains of the *Titanic* were found approximately 375 miles south east of the Newfoundland coast by a joint US–French expedition team led by Dr Robert Ballard of the Woods Hole Oceanographic Institute in Massachusetts and Jean Louis Michel of the *Institut Français de Recherche pour l'Exploitation de la mer* (IFREMER). The research vessel *Knorr* towing a minisub the *Argo* found the wreck, initially sighting a boiler but then locating the front part of the ship, around which lay bottles of wine, anchor chains, a chamber pot and lumps of coal. The ship lay broken up into two main sections on the sea-bed, more than 12,400 feet down beneath the surface. It took five days of filming and exploring before the aft part of the ship was located two thousand feet away from the fore section. Such extreme depths – exerting a water pressure of 6,000 lbs per square inch – required advanced and specialist underwater equipment to locate, sight and film the wreck pieces and the debris between them. This contains twisted and broken pieces of hull, popped rivets, bulkhead plates – as well as more haunting reminders of the last people to walk her decks. There are plates and cutlery from the dining rooms, furniture from the cabins and decks, ceramics, shoes, suitcases and leather sacks. Everything else of an organic origin has long since been recycled into the seabed by the action of bacteria and scavengers. Over the course of this expedition – estimated to have cost in excess of $15 million dollars – and a second visit in July 1986, Ballard and his team took some 60,000 photographs and shot over 60 hours of film of the wreck. Eventually Ballard released the coordinates of the *Titanic*'s location, spread across nearly a mile of sea-bed: the bow section lay at 41° 43' 57" North (of the equator), 49° 56' 49" West (of Greenwich); the boilers at 41° 43' 32" N, 49° 56' 49" W; the stern section almost 2,000 feet away from the bows, at 41° 43' 35" N, 49° 56' 54" W. Interestingly, she was found over 13 miles southeast of the position given by the *Titanic*'s wireless operator in his final distress call (41°46' N, 50° 14' W). Ballard and the team had succeeded on their third attempt where many previous expeditions – some hare-brained and impractical, other more modern efforts well-planned and resourced – had failed. At least ten schemes to find and in some cases raise the *Titanic* were cooked up between 1912 and 1985. Some of the more ridiculous ones included plans to pump the wreck full of Vaseline or molten wax which would harden and become buoyant; a plot to attach huge magnets or nylon balloons onto the hull to drag it up; and encasing the *Titanic* in ice, which would float up (enough ice already, you might well think).

The slumbering giant disturbed
The ethical questions of visiting the wreck

After the expedition in 1985 which made the initial discovery Robert Ballard expressed the hope that the world's most famous wreck would be left alone. Indeed, his expedition had resisted significant pressure to raise objects from the site, and waived 'salvor-in-possession' rights. Concerned by the prospect of looting of the site by organizations with more commercial and less ethical motivation, Ballard and a group of *Titanic* survivors sought the assistance of the US government in protecting the wreck and its remains from salvage. In seeking to give the *Titanic* site protection from what he described as 'wanton grave robbers', Ballard compared the discovery of the wreck to more ancient archaeological wonders: '*Titanic* is like a great pyramid which has been found and mankind is about to enter it for the first time since it was sealed. Has he come to plunder or appreciate? The people of the world clearly want the latter.'

However, having pinpointed the whereabouts of the ship his hope was, predictably perhaps, in vain. Accompanied by much controversy, in 1987 the site was revisited by IFREMER, which had participated in the first successful Ballard expedition. This time IFREMER worked in partnership with a private American company, Titanic Ventures (now RMS Titanic Inc). Together the two 1987 expedition partners removed nearly two thousand artefacts from outside and around the wreck and restored them before being put on display in special exhibitions. Six years later RMS Titanic Inc salvaged several hundred more items from outside the wreck after diving 15 times on it, and has continued to exhibit these internationally.

WHAT ARTEFACTS HAVE BEEN RECOVERED FROM THE SEA–BED SO FAR?
Spectacles, passenger lists, glass bottles, tobacco tins, shoes, clothing, jewellery, soap bars, crockery, cutlery, menus, signage and coins have all been salvaged from the sea floor around the wreck of the **Titanic.**

RMS Titanic Inc's use of surface 'mother' ships deploying remotely-operated underwater vehicles (ROVs), autonomous underwater vehicles (AUVs) and manned mini–subs, at great expense, has permitted access to one of the most hostile environments on Earth and facilitated the capture of detailed imagery of the wreck and the surrounding debris field. According to Ballard, 'there is not a square inch of the *Titanic* that has not been photographed in beautiful detail.' Some argue this is already sufficient intrusion into the maritime grave site. RMS Titanic Inc has already raised relatively large chunks of the hull, and continues to mine the debris field, arguing that the more they find the more the world will understand about the ship and its breaking up. But the dream of raising the *Titanic* will probably never be fulfilled. She is in too poor a state to contemplate trying to bring the biggest sections up to the surface intact. The cost would be phenomenal and likely beyond any commercial venturers.

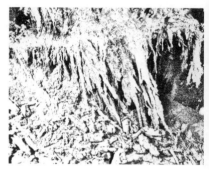

Detached rusticles

THE AUTONOMOUS UNDERWATER VEHICLE

Jam-packed with the latest in submersible technology, the AUV is one of the best ways for explorers to accurately map and record the **Titanic** *site. It contains sonar gear to scan not only what's lying on the sea–bed but also what is hidden beneath in the mud, providing 3-dimensional profiling of any objects it detects. It also uses perhaps the most advanced digital camera ever deployed commercially at sea; equipped with a powerful strobe light acting in the manner of a camera flash, the AUV can hover over the site at an 'altitude' of 10 metres, constantly logging positional GPS and inertial*

navigational data with imagery,
allowing a 'photo-mosaic' of the site
to be built up electronically.

The last survivors
of the *Titanic*
Lillian Asplund and
Millvina Dean

There is no-one left alive today who sailed on the *Titanic*. In June 2009 the last person alive known to have been aboard the *Titanic* passed away in Hampshire. Elizabeth 'Millvina' Dean was a nine-week-old babe in arms in April 1912, travelling from Southampton in Third class with her parents and two-year-old brother Bert. The family were on their way to a new life in Kansas City, where they planned to open a tobacconist's shop. After mother and children were rescued and reached New York the family, then three strong, returned to Southampton where Millvina would spend much of the rest of her life. Millvina was not told of her father Bertram's fate until she was eight years old; her mother Georgetta had been too distraught to speak about it.

Almost an object of fascination to *Titanic* enthusiasts in her own right – even moreso once the wreck of the ship was discovered in 1985 – she was often quick to point out that, quite naturally, she remembered absolutely nothing of the fateful voyage – not the collision, the sinking nor her rescue. Yet she felt connected to the events very strongly. Ms Dean was known to have had misgivings about the exploitation of the wreck site, arguing like many others that it was wrong to disturb the resting place of so many people; she even boycotted James Cameron's 1997 film for fear that it would upset her. Nevertheless she was a willing participant in exhibitions and conventions.

A young Millvina Dean

Unfortunately in later years she reportedly found it hard to make ends meet and decided to sell some of her original *Titanic* mementoes – her canvas mail bag, used to transport the family's belongings back from New York – fetched £1,500 at auction in Devizes. (Ironically, Cameron and his two lead actors, Leonardo DiCaprio and Kate Winslet, each made contributions to her care costs.) She firmly believed that the *Titanic* had profoundly influenced her life – at the very least she was not to grow up an American because of it.

The last known American survivor

Millvina Dean, April 1999

of the disaster was Lillian Asplund, who died in Massachusetts in May 2006, aged 99. Unlike Millvina, Lillian was old enough to have memories of the disaster, in which she lost her father and three brothers (including her twin). Her mother and a fourth brother managed to survive. The family had been travelling back to the US after visiting relatives in Sweden. Lillian seems to have preferred to avoid publicity about the tragedy and rarely spoke about her memories – instead she retired early to take care of her mother Selma, who was said to have found it impossible ever to get over the events of that night.

Titanic sails up the Thames
Tragedy, tourism and trade

In October 1994 Britain's National Maritime Museum in Greenwich was chosen to play first host to the *Titanic* artefacts recovered by RMS Titanic Inc as 'salvor-in-possession', in what quickly became its most popular 'blockbuster' exhibition to date. Over a quarter of a million people visited within six months of opening. Critics – including the world governing body of museums to which the NMM subscribes – were vocal in accusing the museum and the company of 'trophy-hunting' – commercially exploiting a sensitive, vulnerable heritage site and human memorial – and alleging that the salvage was being undertaken without due care and attention to approved archaeological convention. Defending the plan, museum officials assured the public that no artefacts had been obtained from within the wreck itself, only from the sea-bed, and pointed to the need to record the heritage before it rusted into oblivion. Visitors were polled to find out what they thought of national flagship museums displaying artefacts salvaged by commercial ventures from fatal shipwrecks; 70 per cent of the 71,000 respondents believed it was acceptable. Arguably these are people who have already voted with their feet to some extent by electing to visit the exhibition in the first place!

GLOBAL EXHIBITIONS

RMS Titanic Inc's exhibition visited British shores again in 2010–2011, *taking up residence in the London O2 Bubble arena in Greenwich. Featuring 300 artefacts raised from the debris field plus recreations of the* **Titanic***'s First- and Third-class cabins, the boiler room and cargo hold, the company's offerings included new underwater footage of the wreck taken during the most recent of seven previous dives, in the summer of 2010. The exhibition has been seen all over the world, from the Czech Republic, Canada, Brazil and Australia, proving the enduring global fascination with the ship.*

Meanwhile, many other museums, oceanographic institutes, civic centres and tourist attractions around the world have staged *Titanic*-themed exhibitions, often focussing on passengers and artefacts with local connections. One of the most impressive permanent displays can be seen in Belfast's Ulster Folk and Transport Museum, which holds ships' plans and local memorabilia for the *Titanic* along with a collection of more than 7,000 items relating to the ship's parent company the White Star Line and the Harland and Wolff yard.

'Rusticles'
What's eating the Titanic?

At 12,850 feet down on the bottom of the Atlantic, there is almost no oxygen and so you'd be forgiven for thinking that rusting – the oxidisation of iron in the presence of moisture – couldn't occur. But observers of the wreck bring back stories of collapsing decks, wobbly panels and unsafe bulkheads. The ship is falling to pieces. So what's destroying the *Titanic* – once the biggest piece of ironwork on the planet? The answer is: bacteria.

Voracious microbes specially adapted to life in the pitch-black abyss will eventually consume the metal wreckage of the *Titanic* as she is currently situated. In late 2010 Canadian scientists announced that analysis of samples of the 'rusticles' that adorn the wreckage had pointed to the discovery of a new species of bacteria helping to speed up the wreck's disintegration. They named it *Halomonas titanicae* and reported that the ship was being degraded at a pace not previously expected. 'In 1995, I was predicting that *Titanic*

had another 30 years,' Henrietta Mann, adjunct professor with the Department of Civil Engineering at Dalhousie University in Nova Scotia, said in a statement. 'But I think it's deteriorating much faster than that now... Eventually there will be nothing left but a rust stain.'

According to visitors to the wreck – who go down to witness the laying of plaques in memory of the disaster, or to film – the structural integrity of the vessel is fast crumbling, and regular visitors comment how much more of the ship's surface area is covered by rusticles every time they go back. Rusticles are not unique to the wreck of the *Titanic* – other shipwrecks are adorned by them – but thanks to the depth of the wreck there is almost no competition for bacteria from normal marine plant and animal life usually found on wrecks in more shallow waters. The corrosion and decomposition of the ship due to the uninterrupted action of specialist bacteria can occur at a higher rate as a result.

A member of the Canadian research team explained the exponential scale of the risk to

Titanic's fabric: 'The research we have done so far indicates that the bacteria are taking out 0.3 of a gram per centimetre squared per day so that is a lot of iron that is coming out of the ship.' One observer estimated that this equates to approximately 300 kilograms of steel per day, which will increase as the rusticles spread and start to eat into newly-exposed areas.

Some scientists estimate that by the end of the twenty-first century the decks will probably have collapsed into the hull. Others expect this to happen in half the time. One arguably beneficial side-effect is that it is already possible to see into more of the interior than ever before. Cabins, bathrooms, passageways, vestibules, landings and stairwells will slowly be uncovered layer by layer, revealing the much more personal artefacts still lying in the ship. For instance, according to the 2005 report by a BBC Northern Ireland team who visited the wreck to help position a plaque on behalf of Harland and Wolff and the people of Belfast, the enamel bath – complete with taps – used by Captain Smith for his ablutions nearly a century ago is

Titanic's *bow*

clearly visible now that the side of his quarters has collapsed in on itself.

It seems that the giant vessel – once the apogee of man's talent to engineer the natural world to his ends – will be chewed up and spirited away piece by piece by some of the world's smallest organisms. In 250 years the great ship will probably have gone.

Bibliography:

Ballard, R. and I. Coutts, *Titanic: The Last Great Images* (Haynes Publishing, 2007)

Barratt, N., *Lost Voices from the Titanic: The Definitive Oral History* (Arrow Books, 2010)

Beavis, D., *Who Sailed on Titanic? The definitive passenger lists* (Ian Allan, 2002)

Beesley, L., *The Loss of the S. S. Titanic: Its Story and Lessons* (1912)

Brewster, H., and L. Coulter, *882 Amazing Answers To Your Questions About The Titanic* (Scholastic, 1998)

Carey, J. (ed.), *The Faber Book of Reportage* (Faber and Faber, 1987)

Chirnside, M., *The Olympic Class ships: Olympic, Titanic and Britannic* (Tempus Publishing, 2004)

Cousins, M., *The Story of Film* (Pavilion, 2004)

Dawson, P., *The Liner: Retrospective and Renaissance* (Conway Maritime Press, 2005)

Felkins, Leighly and Jankovic, 'The Royal Mail Ship *Titanic*: Did a Metallurgical Failure Cause a Night to Remember?', 50 (1) (1998), *Journal of Metallurgy*

Gardiner, R. *The History of the White Star Line* (Ian Allan, 2001)

Gracie, A., *Titanic: A Survivor's Story* (History Press edition, 2008)

Hackett, C. and J. G. Bedford, *The Sinking of the Titanic: Investigated by Modern Techniques* (The Northern Ireland Branch of the Institute of Marine Engineers and the Royal Institution of Naval Architects, 1996)

Hosty, K., 'A matter of ethics: shipwrecks, salvage, archaeology and museums', *Bulletin of the Australian Institute for Maritime Archaeology*, vol. 19 (1), pp. 33-36

Hutchings, D. F., *RMS Titanic: A modern legend* (Waterfront Publications, 1995)

Lord, W., *A Night to Remember* (Penguin, 1976)

Maltin, T. and E. Aston, *101 Things You Thought You Knew About the Titanic…but Didn't!* (Beautiful Books, 2010)

Shapiro, M., *Total Titanic: the most up-to-date guide to the disaster of the century* (Pocket Books, 1998)

Sinclair, D., *Dynasty: The Astors and their times* (Onslow Books, 1983)

Wheatley, K., *National Maritime Museum Guide to Maritime Britain* (Webb & Bower, 1990)

Web resources:

www.averydeceivingnight.com
www.charlespellegrino.com
www.encyclopedia-titanica.org
www.european-emigration.com/
uk/shippinglines
www.expeditiontitanic.com
www.henry-aldridge.co.uk
www.marconigraph.com
www.maritime.elettra.co.uk/titanic
www.paullee.com/titanic
www.rmstitanic.net
www.southampton.gov.uk/s-
leisure/artsheritage/history/titanic/
www.thegreatoceanliners.com
www.titanicfacts.net
www.titanicinquiry.org
www.titanicuniverse.com
www.titanichistoricalsociety.org

Picture Credits:

p22 yzmo,
p117 Renata3,
p137 Lori Johnston RMS *Titanic*
Expedition 2003, NOAA-OE

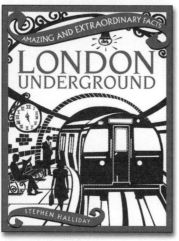

Amazing and Extraordinary
Facts Series: London
Underground
Stephen Halliday
ISBN: 978-1 -910821-039

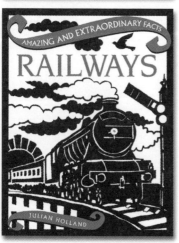

Amazing and Extraordinary
Facts Series: Railways
Julian Holland
ISBN: 978-1 -910821-008

Amazing and Extraordinary
Facts Series: Ireland
Sarah Elliott
ISBN: 978-1 -910821-138

Amazing and Extraordinary
Facts Series: Ghosts
Malcolm Day
ISBN: 978-1 -910821-183

For more great books visit our website at **www.rydonpublishing.co.uk**

INDEX

A Rydon Publishing Book
35 The Quadrant
Hassocks
West Sussex
BN6 8BP

www.rydonpublishing.co.uk
www.rydonpublishing.com

Revised edition first published by Rydon Publishing in 2019
First published by David & Charles in 2012

ISBN: 978-1-910821-19-0

Printed in Poland by BZGraf SA